Sober Vibes

Sober Vibes

A Guide to Thriving in
Your First Three Months *Without Alcohol*

COURTNEY ANDERSEN

Founder of the Online Community Sober Vibes

PAGE STREET
PUBLISHING CO.

PAGE STREET
PUBLISHING CO.

DEDICATION

For Matthew, Fiona and CJ:
Thank you for being my greater WHYs.

And to the soul who is struggling . . .
don't ever, ever give up.

SOBRIETY WILL CHANGE YOUR LIFE

CONTENTS

ONE DAY AT A F*CKING TIME

INTRODUCTION

Hello, my name is Courtney Andersen, and I once had the most intoxicating love affair with alcohol and all the chaos that came with it. My relationship with alcohol started when I was nineteen years old and ended just about six weeks shy of my thirtieth birthday.

My relationship with alcohol started off very innocently, but I knew the moment I fell in love with it. I can remember it like it was yesterday. I lived in the suburbs of Detroit, and Windsor, Ontario was about a twenty-minute drive from there. What was so great was the legal drinking age in Canada was nineteen, so on my birthday we went to Windsor, and it was love at first sip. I immediately felt safe, alive and like I was finally able to come out of my shy shell.

That night, I danced 'til dawn and had one of the best outings of my life. I even felt comfortable enough to lower any fear of flirting and interacting with men. Funny what alcohol allows you to do. That evening started it all.

What I did not know about this new relationship that I had allowed into my life was that it was going to be the most dangerous one of all, and that it would lead to a ten-year rollercoaster of addiction.

At twenty-five, I knew that there was eventually going to be a day when I would have to live a life without alcohol. That's right—I knew it in my soul. I felt it in my gut, and that little voice was saying, "You need to quit drinking." In my opinion, I truly think we all know if we have a problem with alcohol; it just comes down to whether or not we address it.

From nineteen to twenty-five, my relationship with alcohol changed and started to become a lot darker. What was once fun suddenly became doom and gloom. Blackouts were happening more frequently . . . sometimes weekly. During these blackouts, I became uncontrollable and unreasonable. I started noticing that after the first few sips of booze, it felt like a switch was turned on in my head and there was no stopping until I passed out. There was no off switch, and I could not "control" it. I loved drinking myself into a blackout. The times I did not, I often found myself getting pissed, like, "Why am I not drunk enough?" It is hard for me to remember events and the timeline of things during these years. I gauge these times by who was the president of the United States.

My drinking led to many nights of deep fury and lashing out at whoever was around. My drunken rages consisted of yelling and physical altercations. I was even known to throw things. And my hangovers became events—I always drank so much that I would give myself alcohol poisoning.

Some of these nights landed me in the hospital or the local police station. Some of these nights led me to using cocaine and eventually smoking crack a few times. Some of these nights led me to waking up in strangers' beds, not knowing their names and wondering if we had used protection. One of these nights I did say no. I said it more than once and the sexual act continued. What happened to me was wrong. Alcohol or no alcohol, no always means no. It has taken me years to forgive myself for putting myself in dangerous situations while actively addicted. Alcohol and rape culture go hand and hand. With time, therapy and forgiveness, I can say I no longer shame or blame myself for any of these situations I was in.

My drinking led me down the path of self-destruction. I was slowly killing myself. During my active relationship with alcohol, I twice tried to end my life.

From twenty-five to twenty-nine, I tried the moderation game. This game is very exhausting. I would say no to shots, make sure not to mix alcohol, drink wine only, no gin, no whiskey, go a week without drinking, only drink on the weekends, only drink on a Monday, avoid day drinking, only have two drinks when going out, make sure to eat before I drink . . . because we all know *that* was the problem.

This cycle continued, and I tried to control and control and control. The reality was I was past the point of no return. Alcohol had already become problematic in my life and had taken over my brain. Moderation is how "normal drinkers" operate.

I had thousands of rock-bottom moments and was enabled by many around me. The people who enabled me are not bad humans and neither are you if you have been enabling someone. (There is a *lot* to say on that topic.) Even waking up in a hospital bed after a night of drinking didn't make me stop the madness. I really do believe you get to a point in your journey where you just have had enough and can't physically and mentally live in what you are doing anymore. You get good and tired.

My final rock bottom was when I lost my cat, Fiona, for the second time while blacked out. That, and my boyfriend laid out an ultimatum for me that no one had done before. He said, "You can continue to drink, but I will not be here for it."

For three days, I lived in our guest bedroom, dry heaving on the floor and detoxing from alcohol. I only came out to use the bathroom, get food and collect all the beverages to quench my thirst and rehydrate. During this last hangover, I also had to lay in my shame. The shame of all the years of drinking hit me all at once, and it was so overwhelming that it caused anxiety attacks. Trust me, it was not a good time.

Lying in my hangover, I said to the universe, "If I find Fiona and she is still alive, I will give up drinking for good." By the third day, I found her and I have kept my word.

The last night I drank was August 17, 2012. I blacked out that night for the last time in my life, and August 18, 2012, was the first day of the rest of my life.

People always want to know what I did to "get" sober. The answer is this: I made the decision that it was time to quit drinking. I did not allow myself to think about how it was all going to play out. Every day I woke up and said "I am not going to drink." I had to tell myself this some days on repeat.

I used outside help along my journey and recovery, like Alcoholics Anonymous (AA), therapy, coaches, personal development, meditation, breathing exercises, gratitude, leaning into friends and family for support, nutrition, exercise, laughter and online groups. All of these are part of the program I created for myself, and it all eventually led me to create the brand Sober Vibes, which is an online community that supports and empowers sober and sober curious people along their journey.

During those first two years, I white knuckled a lot . . . until I was ready and comfortable to dive deep and figure out why I even drank like I did in the first place. There are many layers to unpack when it comes to this process, and I am a firm believer there is no one way to recover. You have to do what works for you and connect with people you vibe with. That is what I have done since the start.

My sober birthday is by far the most important day in my life, and as I write this book, I am celebrating ten years sober. Insert me dancing in my chair! Not one drop of alcohol. Many doubted me from the start and that is okay, because some days I didn't know if I could do it. But I just kept the focus on getting through another day sober, and little by little days turned to months and months turned to years.

I know without a doubt that the decision to quit drinking alcohol was one that completely changed my life for the better. Since quitting drinking, the gifts of sobriety keep showing up in my life every day.

That boyfriend who presented me with the most powerful decision of my life is now my husband, and we have been together for eleven years and married for seven. Matthew gave up drinking with me. Coming from his own experience and how alcohol played a role in his life, he was at a point where he was over it.

During those first few months of sobriety, we talked about when we would have kids, how we wanted to break the cycle with us and for our children to never experience alcoholism in the home. We welcomed our first child in September 2021, and besides sobriety, he is the greatest gift I have ever received. Alcohol will never be the central focus of his life, and that may be the greatest gift I can give him.

ASSESSING WHY YOU ARE HERE

Why are you here? I need you to be crystal clear about your "why." Sobriety is a journey, and oftentimes we can lose sight of why exactly we needed to sever our connection with alcohol to begin with. As someone who spent four years "moderating" their drinking, I know this firsthand. To start off on the right path, you first need to really, really interrogate why you are here. As your sober coach, I need you to be so transparent about your "why" that, when times of temptation and triggers arise, you understand where alcohol will lead you if you decide to pick up that first drink.

When I first quit drinking, my "why" came from what was most relevant at the time: the physical feelings of being hungover, the shame I felt after telling my boyfriend I was going to kill him and the terrible guilt I felt for losing my rescue cat, again. To this day, I recall the shame and pain of my last hangover because it helps me to not pick up a drink.

Maybe you are here because you have fallen into the parent drinking culture. Yes, it's real. Mommy-and-daddy drinking culture is an epidemic and continues to explode (and it only got worse during the COVID pandemic). Maybe you are a parent who started drinking wine to unwind after the kids went to bed, and you are now waking up wondering how you got to the point of drinking one to two bottles of wine a night.

Maybe you are here because you are the high-functioning drinker who has always been enabled. You hold down a great job, pay your bills on time, support family and work best under pressure, but then you come home and drink yourself to sleep. You are trying to fill a void, and you never feel full.

Maybe you are here because you are the empty nester who comes home to an empty house, and the loneliness you feel is crippling.

Maybe you are here because you are single with zero kids, and you've done what you always wanted to for so long. Choosing the single life yet married to your drinking lifestyle, you wake up at fifty wishing to find love and a life partner.

Maybe you are here because you started drinking after a divorce. After all, you feel like you have some freedom after being married to that smug prick for so long. The freedom feels fantastic, but with this new freedom and finding yourself, your once-a-week wine habit has grown into something uncontrollable.

Maybe you are here because you grew up with a parent or parents who were drinkers, and that's all you were shown, and now in your adult years you're saying: I drink like my mom, or I act just like my dad after a couple of beers. Or you are even realizing some family trauma was your gateway to your alcohol addiction.

Maybe you are here because you have finally hit a rock bottom and are just good and tired. Yes, a rock bottom. As a sobriety coach, I've noticed there is such a preconceived notion about this "hitting rock bottom" moment. I have seen and heard a lot of judgment about it since getting sober, and the funny thing is, it often comes from people who are drinkers. A rock bottom for you could simply mean you are at a point where alcohol no longer serves you. Just because you don't have an extreme case like getting a DUI or resorting to violence, it doesn't mean you can't identify a low point. You are here, reading this book and looking to get help on your sobriety journey—whatever incident caused you to take that plunge. My nine hundred and ninety-nineth rock bottom presented itself as me losing my cat for the second time. Was that the worst thing I did during my active addiction? No. But it was the one where I wanted so badly to get off the ride. I was physically and mentally exhausted at twenty-nine years old.

I've listed many different reasons why someone might be reading this book, and at the end of the day, alcohol doesn't discriminate. Male, female, however you identify and whatever race you are . . . alcohol doesn't care. We are all an open target for the path of destruction alcohol can bring to our lives.

It truly doesn't matter what path led you here; I don't judge and I hope you don't either. We are all having a human experience on planet Earth, and empathy when it comes to this journey is needed—not only for others but for yourself. What matters is that you have chosen to start loving yourself and wanting to live a life without alcohol in it. I'm proud of you for being here and making this choice.

I know you are scared and have lots of questions. You're even thinking about your future self, and wondering how you will ever have fun without alcohol, travel without alcohol or even have sex without a few drinks. I've been there and understand!

Some things I share in this book may not make sense initially. You may ask, "Is doing this exercise going to help me?" and the answer is, yes! These are all things I have done and used in my recovery. They are also what I offer my clients when I coach them through their first few months of sobriety. I'm going to ask you to trust me and trust the process of this journey.

Statistically, 80 to 85 percent of people who start their sober journey relapse. It took me four years to finally say enough is enough. Don't let that discourage you though—you can always be the exception to the rule if this is your first go at quitting drinking.

My coaching is designed to not overwhelm you. I do believe it's very easy to get overwhelmed when it comes to quitting drinking, as we tend to use "getting overwhelmed" as a coping tool. When it comes to this space, overwhelm is not a choice.

Overwhelm often leads to burnout, which leads to relapse. That's why I have broken this book down into three sections, one for each of the first three months of your sober journey, with details on what to focus on during that time. I have also included Coach Tips to help you along the way, as well as homework questions you can answer right in this book.

You cannot rush recovery and healing. It's a process; trust it and trust it from someone who has been there with lived experience. I have not stayed sober since August 18, 2012 by magically hitting a fast-forward button. I've sat in discomfort many days. It's during those days you will learn the most in this process and how fucking strong you are.

Now, let's get started. It's time to dig in and dive into some sober soul-searching. When it comes to your homework, please do what works for you. Not everyone is into journaling their feelings. Maybe you are a painter or you love scrapbooking or you prefer voice memos. Whatever your preferred mode, do what speaks to you. But I do ask you to do the work in this book. Once you read the chapter, do the homework right away. Provide detailed responses, but please do not overwhelm yourself or get caught up in perfectionism. A good practice is to let the thoughts flow, and try to not pause writing (even if the words don't sound perfect). Just get your ideas out and see what comes to the surface. The best part about this book is that there is room to write your responses right in these pages.

Just for a few minutes, I want you to look two years down the road. Close your eyes, take a few breaths and visualize yourself living an alcohol-free life. What and who is around you? How do you feel at this moment? Are you content? At peace? Are you smiling because you know you haven't had a drink in 730 days? Picture and feel it all. When you attach yourself to positive feelings, your outcome will be that.

If you don't believe in yourself, which is very common at this point in your journey, please know that I believe in you, and I'm always in your corner.

COACH TIP

Write out this mantra or say it out loud every day when you wake up: *I choose not to drink today.* It may seem silly to you right now, but we are rebuilding a new you with some positive self-talk. There is a big difference when you say, "I choose to" versus "I can't have something." When "can't" is involved, it sounds like you are being deprived. Quitting drinking is a solid choice and one you have to make daily, so empower yourself and state each day that you choose not to drink.

HOMEWORK

What is your "why" for quitting drinking?

What and how do you feel the next day after a night of drinking? Regret? Shame? Anxiety? Hangovers that last for three days? Write out the next day and how you feel.

What is one action you regret doing in your active relationship with alcohol, and how did it make you feel? If this regrettable action involved a person, how did it make them feel?

Have you tried moderation or sobriety before? If yes, write about these times and what worked best for you.

In 90 days, how do you want to feel as you're living life without alcohol?

IT'S NEVER TOO LATE TO QUIT DRINKING

Before you start diving into the rest of the book, I want to give you a pick-me-up, because I have found many people are stuck in the thought that it's either too late or too early to quit drinking. But I'm here to tell you: It's never too late and it's never too soon to quit drinking! Believing it's too late or too early can be crippling and act as a roadblock as you move forward in your sober life.

I used to think I was too young at twenty-five to quit. I felt this for many years, and it wasn't until I found clarity in sobriety that I realized I was very wrong. Let me tell you this in the most loving way: You are wrong too. I should have quit at twenty-five when my soul was telling me I was going to live a life without alcohol one day.

I ignored my gut for a very long time. Looking back, I can see that I ignored this instinct before my problem even began. I didn't start drinking until I was nineteen, and the reason was because mental health and addiction issues ran in both sides of my family. I had always stuck to not drinking because I was scared I was going to have the same problems. Of course, my gut instinct was right.

Going forward, do not ignore that instinct! This feeling you get will never be wrong. I'm sure there are some moments right now you could look back on and say, "I should have trusted it."

Your gut could have been telling you since you were twenty-five, thirty-five or forty-five that it was time for you to quit drinking, but like me, you ignored it and continue to ignore it. One of the many gifts of sobriety you will receive is that, within time, you will trust and act on that gut instinct a lot more. Get excited for what is to come!

Holding onto the belief that there's a right time or age to quit will keep you stuck in a sick state of being. It's no good. What matters is you are here at whatever age reading this book. I highly doubt you would even be reading such a thing if you were not ready to make a change. The universe works in mysterious ways, and you would not have been ready two, five or ten years ago to make that change. Remember that all of us have that moment where we are finally tired. So maybe at fifty you are good and goddamned tired of this cycle and yourself. You are ready to receive and believe in you and this process of sobriety and healing.

Somewhere along your journey, this little voice came along and started telling you these outrageous stories of how you are not good enough, don't deserve nice things and, my personal favorite, "This is who I am." I say bullshit to it all. During my active addiction with alcohol, the story I continued to create for myself was that I didn't deserve to feel good. I didn't deserve A, B, C and D. Self-sabotage is real and so are limiting beliefs. Let's also add on trauma and the family dynamic you come from, and how those can form a story about how addiction fits into who we are. When you quit drinking, there are a lot of beliefs to let go of, but I know that you can create new ones for yourself.

Right now, I want you to breathe in through your nose and out through your mouth very slowly. Do this two more times. After you're done, I want you to forgive yourself for where you are currently with your drinking. Yes, I know that forgiveness won't make everything better, but this is a start in your process. Let go of the "could've, would've, why-am-I-fifty-and-now-getting-my-shit-together" mentality. These beliefs no longer serve you and are far from empowering. Kiss that thought goodbye. See ya, never want to be ya! Kick rocks, *au revoir, arrivederci.*

I do have one final secret for you: Sober life can happen for you at any age. The opportunity to live life how you want is your choice. I hope you choose now, and I am your biggest cheerleader in this process.

HOMEWORK

What is the story you keep telling yourself about your age and how it is too early or too late for you to quit drinking alcohol?

What proof do you have that it is too early or too late for you to quit drinking alcohol?

Who quit drinking alcohol around your age? What does their life look like? What have they gone on to do? If you don't know a person in your age bracket, search on Instagram or Google "sober celebs" and read how their lives panned out after they got sober. I'm serious, it helps; I did this when I got sober in 2012.

What excites you about getting sober right now?

In your number of years living on planet Earth, what is ONE dream you have always had that you have wanted to do . . . one of your bucket list items?

Remember this is for you only—no comparison, no overwhelm—and if right now you can't think of something, come back to it. But do this work; it helps.

THE FIRST MONTH

We're going to start by walking you through what your first thirty days without alcohol might look like. I'll tell you what to expect physically and emotionally and give you tools and guidance for working through the various rough patches that will pop up. This is the toughest month to go through, but if you're here and reading this book, congratulations! You are making the best decision of your life. Let's dive in.

REMEMBER THAT THE REASON YOU ARE SAYING GOODBYE TO ALCOHOL IS TO MAKE YOUR LIFE BETTER.

INITIAL PURGING, DETOX AND WITHDRAWAL

Here we go! Are you excited? Nervous? Scared? Ready? Whatever you feel right now as you start your sober journey is valid. It's a lot, and I completely understand. I'm here for you. Lean into this book these next few months and let me make this a tad easier for you.

If at any time in this process you relapse, hit a bump in the road or take a step backwards, pick yourself up the following day and try again.

My clients will tell you that you my motto is: "Little by little each day." You can even hear me say on the Sober Vibes podcast, "Trust the process." These mottos hold true. Use them when you need a reminder that it's not easy. It's a victory!

Every day, you will take it one day at a time. You will get through today not drinking, and then do it again tomorrow, and then the day after and then the day after. Before you know it, it's been thirty days, then sixty and then ninety. Share with me on Instagram any one of these milestones! Tag @sober.vibes and let me know. Even at day one, because we all start there; no one bypasses it and it is a huge milestone. Choosing sober life is the best decision you will ever make.

REMOVE ALCOHOL FROM YOUR SPACE

Confused about where to start? You have already started by questioning your relationship with alcohol. Now it's time to physically start by not drinking alcohol today. You will get through today by not drinking, and then do it again tomorrow, and then the day after and then the day after. There is no magic answer besides this. No one is going to be able to do this but you.

Once you've made the decision, it's time to clean out the fridge, cabinets and whatever bar you have in the home. Yes, get rid of it. Why continue to put temptation in your face? I got rid of the alcohol in my home within thirty days. I poured some out and gave some away.

But Courtney, I live with someone who drinks.

This is very common. I suggest asking the person you live with if they are okay not having alcohol in the home. If the answer is no, then ask if they can at least put the alcohol in the garage or basement or even hide it from you. I know hiding it sounds extreme, but some people need this. And don't assume that the person you live with will automatically think of it. When it comes to the sobriety journey (or life, really), assuming is the worst thing we can do. Be assertive and ask. It's okay to ask; your ask is very valid. By asking, you are also setting a new boundary for yourself. Congratulations! It's huge, as boundaries will be one of your greatest tools in your new life.

During this process of purging alcohol, you may even need to take it a step further by packing away the drinking paraphernalia such as glasses, shakers, neon signs, drinking shirts and the 100 beer koozies you have in the home. I'm not saying throw these out yet, because I know there are a lot of memories associated with the beer koozie you got on your tropical vacation. I get all of this. So do what makes you comfortable in this early process. I kept a few wine glasses because, as one of my dearest gal pals used to say, "Always drink from a pretty glass." I agree, as long as it doesn't trigger you.

I also want you to do two other things in your home:

1.   If there is an area of your house that was your "drinking spot," rearrange and feng shui the area. Move the chair around so that it is not directly in front of the TV. Buy a new throw pillow and add it to the couch. Open the windows, and then smudge the shit out of this area. Yes, I'm one of those. Move the Energy! You have been sitting in some stale-ass energy for some time now. So, please trust me on this. Even if you didn't have a drinking chair, pick a room and create something new by rearranging the vibe in it. Why is this helpful? I want your home to be your sanctuary. I want you to feel as good as possible right now. Everyone deserves that.

2.   If there is a project in your home that you have been putting on the back burner for years, please do that one. Cleaning out your closet. Finishing your photo wall project. Installing a new toilet. Painting the guest bedroom. Picking up dog shit. Purging the clothes your kids have outgrown. Why? Because it's going to make you feel better. Plus, it's giving you something to do with your time in the first thirty days. I'm not saying rip the roof off your home, but I'm sure there is some little project in your home right now that you have been putting off because you were too busy with alcohol.

COACH TIP

Trust the process and shoot for drinking half your body weight in ounces of water. Why am I telling you to hydrate? Because you just did some damage to your body, and alcohol dehydrates us. Time to start healing. Plus, hydration is going to help you feel better.

HOW TO TELL PEOPLE YOU AREN'T DRINKING ANYMORE

In the first thirty days, and even prior to quitting drinking, the thought of telling people you do not drink is one that comes up constantly and can be crippling. You don't know what to say, or how to say it—do you tell them ALL about your drinking episodes? And worse, what if you tell them you're going to quit drinking and then drink the next day? *If I fail, they will think I'm this constant loser.*

Sound about right?

The pressure we put on ourselves in this day and age is way too much. It's time to cut it out, start breathing through it and keep telling yourself, "I am doing the best that I can." I wanted to share that with you now because I'm sure you're reeling over how you're going to tell your wine o'clock bestie that you are quitting drinking.

So how do you tell people you are not drinking alcohol right now? You tell them what you're comfortable with in that moment. That's right, do what works best for you.

Here are a few phrases that work, and little white lies will not hurt . . .

- "I am on antibiotics right now, so I'm not drinking."
- "I am on a detox/cleanse right now."
- "I am not drinking alcohol right now."
- "Alcohol is not for me right now in my life."
- "I decided to give up alcohol right now; I would love your support."
- "I am choosing not to drink alcohol right now; because I have a problem with it. NO shame."

And you don't need to announce it to the world on day one if it's not your thing. Plus, you may have already stated to people five years ago you were going to quit and you continued to drink. I was that person. People did not think I would last. I'm serious. Even my boyfriend (now husband) couldn't believe it. I actually didn't think it myself, but here I am. It's surprising what we can do once we set our minds to something.

Did you notice I also said "right now" when it came to telling someone you weren't drinking alcohol? I didn't say FOREVER. I didn't say "forever" because we don't know if it's going to be forever. Forever is a very scary thought right now. People are going to ask, "So are you not drinking at all anymore, or for good?" Your response should just stay in the now. Still, to this day, and if you hear me on the Sober Vibes podcast, I say today I'm not drinking. Even at ten years sober, we just don't know what life will throw at us.

I will share that this anxiety you feel is a bigger deal to you than it is to the other person. It's also scary because your sobriety is becoming real and the accountability is kicking in. You're going to be met with support 90 percent of the time, or even a person who states they have been thinking about giving up drinking as well. Or that their spouse or parent gave up alcohol years ago and gets it. It will happen. You've got this!

COACH TIP

Do not overthink this. The overthinking and analyzing will drive you nuts. I know this is going to sound ridiculous, but practice what you're going to say before you say it. Yes, role-play by yourself. No shame here. I've done this with many clients and this shit works. You are rehearsing so, when the time comes, you feel more confident in what you're going to say.

DETOX/WITHDRAWALS

Detox is going to happen when you quit drinking. Before I go further, I don't know your true daily habits with alcohol. I was always the person who lied about how much I drank even when I was asked at doctors' visits. I would usually say five to seven drinks a week, which meant fourteen to twenty –plus with some lines of cocaine sprinkled in. I suggest being as honest as possible here because detoxing from alcohol can be severe, and it is one drug that can lead to death when withdrawing from it.

I'm not saying this to scare you, but I believe in sharing facts. I also don't want you to take this information and use it as an excuse to continue drinking, which I've heard from many people before. I strongly recommend talking to your doctor about detoxing from alcohol, if needed. There is no shame here. Don't feel weird either when talking to medical professionals. I used to work in the medical field at a pain clinic, and doctors are a lot more understanding when the patient is being honest. Honesty wins every time.

According to the book *Staying Sober: A Guide for Relapse Prevention*, there are two stages of withdrawal. The first is called acute withdrawal and lasts for three to ten days.

Acute withdrawal symptoms can look like tremors, anxiety, nausea, vomiting, headache, increased heart rate, sweating, irritability, insomnia and high blood pressure. These symptoms can start after around six hours to three days. Many understand this as a hangover, depending on your spectrum of alcohol consumption.

The long-term withdrawal is called post-acute withdrawal syndrome, which is also known as PAWS.

Post-acute withdrawal symptoms look like the inability to think clearly, memory problems, emotional overreactions or numbness, sleep disturbances, physical coordination problems and stress sensitivity. PAWS occur usually within seven to fourteen days and can last up to two years.

Your mind, body and soul are going to take some time to heal. Be patient with it and yourself. One of the best memes I've ever seen states, "Your body is not Amazon Prime. It takes more than two days to get from it what you want." Remember: Straight poison went into your body for years, and there will be some effects from it. What is beautiful about the human body is the amazing ability it has to heal.

COACH TIP

Rest is key during this time. You may be more tired than usual, so when you can, rest your body, even if it's just lying down for an hour when you have time. During states of rest, I highly encourage you to take that time to just rest. No distractions from your phone. One of my favorite resting techniques is to take a shower and then lie in my bed with my robe on and a towel on my head. I call this towel time. It reminds me of a little spa time. I usually just lie in my bed and stare at the ceiling. It's relaxing and gives me a little rest. Sounds silly, but try it. I swear by it.

Take it a step further and nap.

CRAVINGS

The itch, witching hour or the pits are some of the things I used to call cravings.

They will happen, and it's one of those things you will never be able to skip in this process. I'm sorry. I wish we could, but we can't. For some people, as soon as they quit drinking they stop having cravings, but most will experience them. Working through them will only make you stronger.

A majority of cravings come around the time you did your drinking. Or they start a few hours beforehand. Usually, a craving lasts anywhere from seven to twenty minutes. So, when a craving comes up, it's important that you work through it right away. Working through them right away helps you not feed into the romanticized story you have with alcohol and how it solves everything. It doesn't. And I'm here to remind you that alcohol sells a whole lot of lies.

Below are tips to help you get through periods of cravings. Do you need to do them all at once? No, of course not, but I wanted to give you an array to pick from so you have them in your toolbox.

1. Breathing techniques. I'm a huge fan of square breathing (also referred to as box breathing.) It's four counts of breathing in, four counts of holding your breath, four counts of exhaling and four more counts of holding after your exhale. It's an easy concept to grasp when your mind goes into a tad bit of panic. Other breathing techniques you can use include 4-7-8 breathing, pursed lip breathing and diaphragmatic breathing. These techniques can all be found on YouTube.

2. Do something during the craving. Brush your teeth, drink water, pray, play with your dog or cat, chew gum, journal, color, move your body (like walking), have a dance party with yourself, phone a friend/family member to ask how they are doing. Why ask a person how they're doing during a craving? Because it gets you out of your own mind and thoughts. The conversation becomes about someone else and makes you focus on that instead of wanting a drink.

3. Create an affirmation for yourself during this time and repeat it out loud. "I am a strong motherfucker, and I will not drink today." Yes, you can take out the f-bomb.

4. Recite your "why" out loud, or sit down and write it out. You can return to the portion of this book where you wrote out your "why" and read that (page 19).

5. Play the tape in your head of what it would look like if you drank al-cohol. What would tomorrow look like? How would you feel? Who would be disappointed in you? Do you want to wake up hungover? Was the drink worth the feelings you'll feel twenty-four hours from now? You will never want a drink after you play this tape forward.

Number four and five are great practices because you are creating a mindful awareness of what happens when you drink alcohol. It is a beautiful thing because it helps you in the long game of sober living.

Finally (and it's not really a tip), some cravings will pop up, and all of those strategies might fly out the window because of whatever circumstance you are in. You might just have to ride the craving out and let that be the way through. See it as part of the process—try not to fight it or be so fearful of it.

Let me remind you of how strong of a human you are. You can do hard things.

COACH TIP

You are going to notice that with alcohol cravings also come cravings for sweets. A majority of people who quit alcohol catch a sweet tooth. Ride the wave. It will settle in time. Do not be hard on yourself if you start gaining a few pounds. Choose one battle at a time. Would you rather be five pounds lighter with a drinking problem or five pounds heavier, sober and thriving? Choose your "hard." Your "hard" right now is not drinking alcohol.

IT GETS HARDER BEFORE IT GETS EASIER

You are about to endure some difficult and challenging days. I will not sugarcoat this. I believe in honesty and shooting straight. Some days the urge and the "fuck it" attitude are going to be at the forefront of your mind, but I root for you to give it one more day.

When you are in the self-sabotage mindset, I encourage you to not start thinking it's going to be like this every day, and then spiral, thinking of how it's going to be in a year. I ask you to continue to trust me in this process and just know that the first thirty days of quitting drinking are the hardest and most uncomfortable.

Change is hard. It is always difficult before it gets easier. There will be days you will have zero problems and lie in your bed and say, "today was easy" and breathe a sigh of relief. Acknowledge these days and be grateful for them.

COACH TIP

How you are currently feeling is not how you are going to feel in six months. Sobriety doesn't feel like this forever. It gets better, but right now you have to go through the hard part. To start feeling better mentally now, you must lean into gratitude. Every day you wake up sober, say out loud, "I am grateful for another day sober". Double points to you for writing it down each day. Gratitude is key.

HOMEWORK

To-Do List

☐ Talk to your doctor about withdrawal/detox.

☐ Purge the koozies and alcohol paraphernalia.

☐ Get rid of alcohol in the home. Empower yourself by pouring it down the drain, throwing it out or giving it to a friend.

☐ If you live with someone who drinks, find a mutual place to store alcohol that is out of sight and out of mind.

☐ Hydrate every morning before you do anything else. Drink 8 to 10 ounces of water with a dash of pink Himalayan salt in it. Water before the coffee, always.

If you are having a hard time letting go of alcohol by pouring it down the drain or giving it to a friend, write out why below. Why are you holding onto it?

What is the tool of choice you will use to get through cravings? Write out one idea in depth or make a list.

How will you allow yourself to have a little extra rest each day? An hour nap? Quiet time with no distractions? If you have your own idea, write it below. Describe what the scene would look like.

_____

_____

_____

_____

_____

_____

_____

_____

_____

_____

_____

_____

_____

_____

_____

_____

_____

_____

_____

_____

_____

ALCOHOL IS POISON, AND MILLIONS HAVE A PROBLEM WITH IT. LEAVE BEHIND THE THOUGHT THAT YOU ARE NOT NORMAL BECAUSE YOU HAVE AN ISSUE WITH ALCOHOL.

RELEARNING HOW TO LIVE WITHOUT ALCOHOL

A big first step in adjusting to life without alcohol is getting comfortable asking for help. I understand how difficult asking for help can be. I was a person who never asked for any help . . . ever. It was something that I learned from a very early age. It's a blessing and a curse on so many levels. Especially in later years when I needed help the most. It was always after the problem that I would be asked, "Why didn't you ask for help?" The inner rage would boil when I was asked this because I could never say, "I was conditioned to not ask for help." I was always told no, or the favor was always held over my head to make sure I continued to play the role of the good girl in my family. We all play a role in our family dysfunction. When you are raised in a home with mental illness and addiction, it's never about the child and their needs. It creates a dynamic where the child has to fend for themself and become extremely independent.

Maybe you were conditioned to not ask for help. Or maybe you fall in the category of not asking for help because the shame and guilt of your drinking issue are so crippling and you don't want to blow up the "everything is perfect" facade. Or maybe you were conditioned to think getting help was weak. Wherever you fall in the asking for help category, it's time to let go of these old conditions and beliefs. You have the power in your life right now. No one else but you, and you can rewrite a whole new story for yourself.

UNDERSTANDING ALCOHOL CULTURE

We live in a world that is so heavily influenced by alcohol. Alcohol is its own culture and one that millions buy into every day. It's ingrained into our everyday life. It's shocking once you do get sober to see how influenced you and so many others are by it.

Alcohol is the only drug we must explain not using. The ONLY ONE! Why do you have to constantly explain to people that you aren't drinking? No one questions heroin, crack, cocaine and oxycontin. But alcohol? Man, oh man, people can't fathom why someone wouldn't want a drink. It would be terrible to snort lines of cocaine in front of everyone at the family Christmas party, but it's okay for you to be crushing bourbon because it's the holidays and you deserve a drink.

An excellent documentary about alcohol is called *Prohibition* by Ken Burns. It explains the history of alcohol and the impact it has had on our culture. Problems have always been there with people and booze. I watched this during my early sobriety, and it shined a light for me, so watch it if you can. Big Alcohol has been around for years and years and years. The forces behind Big Alcohol are powerful corporations and have been selling lies for decades.

Because of the deep impact of alcohol's role in our society and the delusion it creates, what happens when you are struggling? You can be faced with total and absolute shock from people. *What do you mean you have a problem? You don't look like someone who is an alcoholic. But you're a doctor? Can you just have a couple and just not get too fucked up?* The list goes on.

The reaction comes from a lack of education, the enormous amount of fantasy the media has placed on alcohol throughout the years and the unrealistic picture it has painted of people with drinking issues. Have you ever noticed that no characters in TV shows and movies come home after work and drink sparkling water? It is always an alcoholic beverage, and they function while drinking a whole bottle of wine by themselves. Then, of course, the people with problems that are shown are just an extreme mess. Facts. Yes, there is always an extreme. I wish the media showed functioning alcoholics. People who get up and have to have a drink to level out and then go teach middle school, or the ones who are CEO's and doctors. There are more functioning alcoholics than ones living on the streets.

COACH TIP

Right now I want you to forgive yourself for being influenced by Big Alcohol. It's easy to have fallen into the trap; the t-shirts, the cups, all of it. Alcohol companies need warning labels just like big pharma. The "drink responsibly" is insulting and borderline manipulative.

ASK FOR HELP

Right now, you have to put aside the ego, shame and childhood conditioning and dig deep to ask for help. In the next chapter, I will share more about options for help and support you can lean into. But now it's crucial for you to ask for the help you need and want. Sobriety is something you can of course do on your own, but having help will make it 110 percent easier.

For two years, I white knuckled my sobriety. I went at it alone. Yes, I had my boyfriend for support, but he didn't get what it meant to have anxiety on a Friday night at dinner because all I could do was think about drinking, or that Friday was a huge trigger for me in general, or the sometimes-gut-wrenching urges to drink. I sat in silence and needed help outside of myself.

I became a coach and created courses and resources for you to not have to go through what I did. I wish I made it easier for myself, but what you don't know, you don't know, and you learn from it. Please, learn from me. Make it easier on yourself.

COACH TIP

Affirmations are going to be your friend right now; here are three to use when it comes to letting go of ego and allowing yourself to get help.

- I allow myself to be helped in my sober life.
- Help is needed, and I am here for it.
- I am not weak because I need help.

CONNECT TO YOUR WHY

Now that you are going to lean into getting help, there is one important thing you need to burn into your soul before moving on: Why?

Yes, why.

I touched a little on identifying your "why" before, and we are going to touch on it again. That is how important it is. Why do you want to live a life without alcohol? Why are you giving it up? Who (kids, spouse, your parents) comes into play in that "why"?

For example: My "why" at the time was because I was sick of the cycle, I was exhausted at twenty-nine years old, I knew alcohol was slowly killing me and that it was time. My "why" was my rescue cat, Fiona, and boyfriend, Matthew. The shame wrapped up in losing Fiona twice and hurting someone I loved. The shame cycle was crippling. My hangover anxiety turned into panic attacks . . . why continue doing this to myself?

My "why" today has changed. My "why" today is wrapped into the sweet goodness of my son. I never want him to grow up witnessing a parent with a problem with alcohol. I never want him to ask me one day why I always chose alcohol over him. I want to be present, stable and loving for him. I can't do that if I'm drinking.

Even if your "why" is not people, you need to ask yourself how you want to live your life. Are you currently living that way? I knew at twenty-nine that I didn't want to be living the way I was. You have written down your "why" earlier in this book (page 19). Return to it and read it every day. I want you to take it a step further and write it out in a few places. On a notepad, sticky note or pieces of paper, and stick them where you can see them each day. Stick your "why" on your bathroom mirror, so when you are brushing your teeth you can read it to yourself. Or place a sticky note in your car, so you can read it to yourself at a red light. I don't care how painful it might be; you must write this out, and then read it to yourself out loud. Yes, speak it. Even if tears are rolling down your face, read it out loud. Every day.

I've been asked multiple times throughout my sobriety how I have stayed sober, and the answer always goes back to my "why." I wasn't kidding when I said earlier to burn it into your soul. You will need to keep it close in the next ninety days when you need it most.

COACH TIP

You are not figuring out right now "why" you drank in the first place. That could be a whole list of things that might take some time to unpack. You are focusing on WHY you are quitting alcohol.

TRIGGERS

I won't lie to you: You are going to face triggers throughout your sobriety journey. I want you to first take into consideration that just because you stop drinking doesn't mean the urge isn't going to be there when triggered. I once had a woman tell me during one of my workshops that the limes in the fridge were a trigger for her. I was amazed by this because, honestly, I had never heard of this trigger before, but it makes sense! Goes to show how we are all not the same.

Triggers can be people, places and things. I have always been triggered by people and places.

What do you think yours are? Sometimes you don't even know until you are sober and clarity starts to rise to the surface. If you can't think of it now, give yourself some time, and it will start showing itself.

I didn't realize I was triggered by people until somewhat into my sobriety journey. I went out to dinner with someone and realized mid-bite why I always slammed red wine around this person. It was a real eye-opener, and of course, when I was driving home, the thoughts flooded in of why this person was a trigger for me. In time, healing, boundaries and forgiveness have helped. Today, I have a great relationship with this person and know how to navigate our relationship.

You can't avoid places unless you plan on avoiding life altogether, and I don't want you to. You aren't getting sober to not live life. Trust me, it's worth it. It's normal if places happen to be your trigger, like restaurants, grocery stores, your house and even work. You are not alone in this.

Things may be your trigger, like the woman who shared about the limes. Things you could be triggered by are changes of seasons, culinary experiences, social media, holidays, the news and past trauma. There is more of course, but these are notorious examples that are linked to and associated with drinking alcohol.

When it comes to triggers, you will have to just work through the ones you have zero control over. To this day, when the seasons change, I always think about smoking cigarettes and drinking on a patio. It's just one of those things for me. I think about it when the moment comes up, and then I tell myself out loud, "But I'm glad I don't do those things anymore" and move on. I'm not crippled by it like I once was. It's a thought that goes away within seconds. Identifying your triggers doesn't make them go away, but you'll be prepared for when they come up. And when the urge hits, you might be able to identify more easily what caused this feeling and walk away.

COACH TIP

Really think about what your five top triggers are. Don't just say, "Everything triggers me," because that is not true. The more specific you get with figuring the triggers out, the more you can figure yourself out in the process. Plus, it helps with relapse prevention.

BOUNDARIES

Boundaries and triggers go hand in hand. Boundaries are such a layered topic, which is why I'm recommending another book for you to read after this one. It's called *Set Boundaries, Find Peace: A Guide to Reclaiming Yourself* by Nedra Glover Tawwab. It's the best book I have ever read about boundaries. Tawwab explains so many different situations and how to start setting boundaries. She is brilliant.

When it comes to triggers and boundaries, you will learn how to set boundaries by identifying the people, places and things that trigger you. (I wasn't kidding when I said they go hand in hand.) Also, you may be lacking boundaries or don't even know how to set them because you never saw or never were taught boundaries growing up. I would guess you most likely don't have many, with others or yourself.

Even saying you're going to quit drinking and then drinking again the next day is breaking a boundary within yourself. The good news is that you can change this all around. The first boundary you are going to make and set is within yourself, and that is not drinking alcohol today.

Here are examples of how you can start setting boundaries with people, places and things that trigger you. By setting these boundaries, you are slowly going to condition yourself in a positive way to not be triggered as time goes on.

- Decrease time spent around people who trigger you, even if that includes close family. Instead of three hours with your mother or father, decrease the time to one hour.
- Decrease time spent on the phone or texting with people. Is talking to your mother for two hours too much? Do you feel drained afterwards and like you just rehashed your childhood trauma? Limit phone time and how much you chat with triggering people per week.
- Decrease social media usage. Set timers on your phone for app usage, deactivate your account or delete apps from your phone and only allow yourself to use your computer to access it. I did this with Facebook in 2021, and it's been a game changer! Honestly, I've done all of the above with social media, and it's helped so much. I respect the machine that is social media, but I also have to respect myself more. If I ever feel the triggered, comparison, anxious game come up, I know it's time to put more boundaries in place.

- Remove yourself from certain social settings for a bit. For example, if you are trying to quit drinking, stop going to a bar.
- Order groceries online and pick them up instead of going into the store and being triggered walking down the alcohol aisle.
- Unsubscribe to emails you no longer wish to receive. This just feels good to do!
- Stop watching shows that center on alcohol and partying. In my first ninety days of sobriety, I binged-watched *Friday Nights Lights* because my reality TV smut was too much to handle with the amount of drinking shown. I needed something wholesome, and Coach Taylor and the gang filled this need.
- If fruit in your fridge is a trigger (like a lime), stop buying them for a bit and substitute with lime juice.

When you start eliminating triggers in your life and putting up boundaries, you have a lot more control over yourself and how you react to triggers. You can't control others, but you can control you. The sooner you start implementing boundaries, the better off you will be. You don't need to be perfect here, but you have to start practicing. Consistency over perfectionism always wins.

COACH TIP

You will take three steps forward and five steps back sometimes when creating boundaries. It's okay; give yourself grace. This is a lot of change at once, and it's very easy to fall back on behaviors because it feels comfy to you. If you let a boundary slide, recognize how you feel afterwards. Once you get the momentum of feeling good mentally, you know you don't want to go back to the behavior.

HOMEWORK

Is asking for help hard for you? If yes, why?

_____

_____

_____

_____

_____

_____

_____

_____

_____

_____

_____

_____

_____

_____

_____

_____

_____

_____

_____

_____

_____

_____

_____

_____

_____

Why are you deciding to give up alcohol? Yes, write it out again and get into all the details.

What is the feeling you get the day after drinking?

What people, places and things trigger you? Pick your top five, write them out and reflect on why.

What are ten things you can do to handle a trigger? List five small things and five big things. For example, you could drink water or go for a walk.

Write out the boundaries you've tried to set in your life so far.

_____

_____

_____

_____

_____

_____

_____

_____

_____

_____

_____

_____

_____

_____

_____

_____

_____

_____

_____

_____

_____

_____

_____

What boundaries do you now need to implement in your sober life?

In case I haven't told you, I believe in you, and I'm proud of you for doing this work. I know it's not easy, but it will make sense one day to you.

PEOPLE WHO DON'T SUPPORT YOU NOT DRINKING ALCOHOL ARE CALLED ASSHOLES.

BUILDING A SUPPORT NETWORK

When I quit drinking, there were no Instagram pages, sober Facebook groups, TikTok accounts, podcasts, blogs or massive selection of quit lit and nonprofit organizations dedicated to sobriety and recovery.

My only options for help were rehab and twelve-step programs. Well, twelve-step programs were my only option. Rehab was never on the table for me. Let me first say, I never asked for help because, as I shared with you earlier, I was conditioned not to. But also, I was scared. I feared being told no and carried the shame from all the years of my actions in my active addiction. Also, did I think I needed rehab? I'm sure parts of me during some years of my addiction did. But towards the end, I did not. I believed I could do it on my own. My family never stepped in and said I needed help. Throughout the years, each one said something at some point but never as a collective whole intervention style. I do have to say that the older I got in my active addiction the less and less I would be around family members. Isolation and not engaging is real when it comes to addiction. Family dynamics are tricky and the only person who can get a person sober is the person with the problem.

What's amazing in today's world is that there are so many people sharing their journeys of sobriety and recovery. There are organizations out there connecting people in sobriety with activities or even sober spaces at events. You can press play right now on about ten different sober podcasts. You can even celebrate with thousands of others every year on September 14, which is National Sober Day. Fun fact, I founded this holiday!

The stigma of addiction, alcoholism and alcohol abuse disorder is slowly lifting, and there is no better time to quit drinking than right now.

Support is key when it comes to the journey of sobriety. For so many years, a majority of us were isolated. Isolated in our own drinking and feelings. Drinking becomes extremely isolating not only in action but also as our emotions continue to get buried, and eventually we become very shut off and withdrawn. When you are in your active relationship with alcohol, you are not a present person. If you think no one notices, they do. They just don't say anything because, possibly, you conditioned them not to. Or they just don't have the tools to bring it up.

Support is needed because you need the accountability and help.

Yes, you must be accountable to someone else besides yourself. Did that last sentence give you the feels? I hope so, because if it shook you a bit, it was supposed to. Enabling has been your friend. Your wife, partner, sister, father, friend, mother and brother may have been enabling you for years. If they have, it's okay. We all have been enabled. I was for years. There are so many layers in this field. People don't know the "how to" of stopping enabling you. Maybe they witnessed enabling when they were growing up and are now just repeating the same pattern their mother did. Or maybe they have said something and tried for years to get you to stop drinking and you just don't care enough and haven't stopped yet.

Whatever the case may be, what matters is that as you read this, you know now it's time for a change and it's time for support and accountability.

I'm going to share ways to build up your support network in your alcohol-free journey. Do you need to tap into all of them? That is your decision, but I suggest trying them all or at different times. Also, you should try a few times. Sometimes you will not connect the first time; it might take a few tries. Don't base a decision off what you have heard or think. Take what you want and leave the rest when it comes to all avenues of help. Do what makes you feel good and speaks to you. What works for Sally may not work for Harry.

The idea that there is only one way to recover and get sober is insane . . . seriously. An outdated thought. We aren't prescribed the same medication in the same dosage. This is no different. The goal is always to go to bed another night sober, and how you got there that day is your business.

TWELVE-STEP PROGRAMS

Twelve-step programs are a wonderful place to start at any time!

Twelve-step programs are defined as a group of programs supporting recovery from substance addictions, behavioral addictions and compulsions. Twelve-step programs were formed in 1935, and the first one was Alcoholics Anonymous (AA).

AA has helped many get sober and start the process of recovery.

Meetings are a wonderful way to connect with people in real life and listen to how alcohol has impacted their lives. You may sit there and totally see yourself in the person sitting across the table from you that you just met after listening to their story. It's powerful.

Working the program and finding a sponsor are huge steps forward in the process of recovery. Maybe meetings aren't currently your thing right now, but that doesn't mean down the road they won't be. What's wonderful about twelve-step programs is that the door is always open.

I tried a few meetings during my first weeks of sobriety, and I did not connect with it. Also, at the time, "god" talk was not my bag. If this has happened to you, it is totally normal. That first year, I did read *The Big Book*, as it was recommended to me at my first meeting. *The Big Book* is the basics of AA and the promises found within. It's the literature that goes along with the program. It was helpful and insightful at the time.

I went back to AA during my fourth year of sobriety for a summer and worked the rest of the steps I needed to. I'd made my amends already with the people I needed to on my first sober anniversary. (Making amends is a step in AA. This is where you take accountability for your actions to people you have hurt or wronged.) I specifically waited for my first-year anniversary, so I would be taken seriously by the people I made my amends to . . . so they could see over the last year how I had changed. It was not just another she-didn't-drink-for-ten-days-here-comes-the-apology instance. Plus, that one-year mark for me was huge, and it took me some time to see how my actions in my active relationship with alcohol had affected people. I wanted them to know that my apology was backed by changed action. Why am I telling you this? Because I never suggest doing something if I have not done it myself. I stick by it.

When I went back to AA that summer, I sat at a women's table every Wednesday and connected in person with females who had drinking problems just like me. Listening to the emotional struggles that these women were going through helped me so much because I was going, or had gone, through the same. It is an understanding you do not get from people who don't have issues with alcohol. Being in this environment became healing for me.

What is amazing about AA is the in-person community and support, so even if it's not right for now, maybe it will be some time in the future.

That summer I spent in AA is where the idea for Sober Vibes formed. I listened to what women needed and even what I needed in recovery. We all needed more. I heard it and felt it. I appreciated my time in AA; I took what I wanted and left the rest.

Besides just AA, there are other alternative meetings like SMART Recovery, Women for Sobriety and Recovery Dharma. And Sober Vibes, of course, has monthly meetings. There are tons of options out there, and it just takes a little digging on the Internet to find them.

If you have gone to a few meetings, and they are not your thing, it is okay. There are other tools out there for you. What worked for your bestie may not work for you. You might not vibe, that might not be the type of support you need right now. It's cool . . . no stress. There are other options out there.

COACH TIP

When it comes to twelve-step programs, give it a few meetings and find the one that you connect with. If you're new to AA, know that you will walk into a lot of meetings where people are sitting together at tables. So you might sit at a table you don't connect with, and that is okay. You just might have to find another table to sit at another day. It feels like you're back in middle school, but know that everyone who has walked through those doors was once where you are today. If you sit at a table you really vibe with, keep going to that meeting and sitting with that group. Don't judge twelve steps by what you've heard or what you assume. The meetings are a wonderful tool and a huge resource to lean into.

THERAPY

I love therapy. LOVE.

Therapy is like a warm, soft blanket . . . a totally safe space to talk it out, and maybe even talk about things you've avoided for years!

Everyone in today's world needs therapy. I really do believe it.

There is no shame in the therapy game. To this day, when I hear someone knock therapy, it makes me giggle. And when I have asked if they've ever gone it's a "no, I don't need that shit" kind of answer.

Therapy and I have been kicking it since the mid-nineties. I was a depressed teenager and had my own backpack of different traumas. Every Monday, I looked forward to my therapy sessions. It was a safe space to talk about my feelings, and my first therapist was helpful. As I write this, a memory just came up about how my dad used to pick me up after my therapy sessions and we would go to dinner, just us. Funny how it's easy to forget things as you get older. Some of the best quality time I had with my dad were those Monday nights!

I had one therapist suggest I quit drinking, and I stopped going after that. I really liked her, but she was onto my tricks. She knew. Soon after that therapist though, I would quit drinking.

In my recovery, I have leaned on therapy a lot and used it as part of my program. Therapy has been my lifeline. Usually when people quit drinking, there are some underlying mental health issues, which are perfect for working out with a therapist.

I've noticed that for each year of my sobriety there has been something new I need to work on or figure out from my past. Or even something like being a new mom or the heaviness of the world post-2020. Processing it with a therapist and having a safe space to talk is what's needed. Lots of layers in sobriety!

There are tons of therapists who specialize in addiction. A great website to find one around you is psychologytoday.com. Type in your location and see all the ones that come up and what they specialize in. I also love this website because therapists' pictures are shown. I found my therapist before I quit drinking this way, and I thought "she looks nice and understanding." Most therapists will do a consult and get your history. I suggest doing one first and seeing if you vibe with the person. It's possible you won't, and that is okay, it's nothing to take personally or to discourage you from continuing your therapy journey. Find another one! Also, please don't stay with a therapist you don't vibe with because you feel bad. People pleasing is so last season of your life, which is the one you were drinking in. Remember to let your therapist know about your issue with alcohol and how you have entered the world of sobriety and recovery. The more honest you are with them, the better you will be in the end.

If therapy gives you a scary feeling because it makes you nervous to sort things out, it's okay. Your feelings are valid and normal. Change isn't easy, but working through it will only help you out in the long run and help you gain more tools to cope without alcohol.

COACH TIP

If you can, do something for yourself after your therapy appointment, such as seeing a movie, taking yourself out to eat, grabbing a cup of coffee, getting some ice cream, getting a massage or going to an exercise class. Make this experience enjoyable. I'm here to help you thrive, and doing something after therapy that's enjoyable and decompressing will help. Like my therapy journey in my teens, going out to eat with my dad after was fun. It gave me something to look forward to.

COACHES

The boom in sober/recovery/life coaching has been amazing! Why? Because now there are even more options for help and support. More tools and resources are a blessing, and why not learn from someone who has been where you are now?

There is a big difference between therapists, sponsors and coaches. Let me break them down.

Therapists focus more on mental health and emotional healing, while coaching focuses on setting and achieving goals and supporting you with accountability. Coaches are not sponsors. Sponsors are mentors in a twelve-step program who help guide you through step work. I want to clarify this because coaching services are completely different than sponsors and therapists.

Coaching has played a huge part in my sobriety in many ways. I have worked with two coaches and gained so much knowledge and insight from them. They helped me in that season of my journey, by giving me tools to help with limiting beliefs and mindset (we talk about this in The Second Month; page 77). They even pushed me to get out of my own damn way. Yes! I was the one holding me back when it came to certain things like holding on to negativity and hurt for way too long.

I am a person who works well with a coach. I will always be a person who needs accountability, and working with a coach takes me to my next level. Take that into consideration on your sober path. Maybe you are a person who needs that extra accountability.

Around year six of my sobriety, I decided to become a coach myself. I found this is where my passion was in helping others on their journey. I became a health and fitness coach during year three and loved it. Since I was loud and proud in my recovery, I would have people reach out for help all the time. It was important to me to wait to become a sober coach and not jump into it too soon. Why? Because I needed to work through my own baggage before I dove into others.

If you'd like to work with a sober coach in addition to using this book, search Instagram, type in sober coach and see how many come up! And of course, I offer coaching programs for thirty days and eight weeks as well as one-on-one mentorship for three months to a year.

I found this funny, but sober coaches always get the "fraud" rap. I've worked with many clients who told me their friends warned them to watch out because they heard sober/recovery coaches were all a scam and just want your money. I'm not kidding. You may have heard this as well. Yes, of course anything nowadays could be a fraud. You know how many people I hear say their sponsor ghosted them, that they smelled alcohol on their therapists, and that rehabs have become crooked? So, here are my tips when it comes to finding a coach if you decide to go this route. Ask these questions:

- How long have you been consistently sober?
- What avenues of help have you received?
- Do you guarantee sobriety?
- What boundaries do you set with a client?
- Do you offer medical advice?

Why these questions?

- Because the length your coach has been sober matters when it comes to your journey, honestly. Do you want someone coaching you who is newly sober or is just coming off a relapse? One year is still very early in recovery.
- Dear God, please ask about the help they've received. I have known people in this space who have journaled as their form of help. Yes, journaling is a tool and helps one reflect. Getting help outside of yourself is KEY, though. I know the coaches I have worked with (and even myself) have sought help in all different avenues. If they just quit drinking and think that's plenty, it's not. I'm sorry, it's not. Yes, you stopped, but it doesn't mean you are a healthy person.

- If anyone guarantees you sobriety, the red flags should instantly pop up. No one, not even god herself should be telling you they can guarantee you sobriety. I have said to every one of my clients in a consult call that I cannot guarantee them sobriety. I can't be there and physically slap chardonnay out of your hands, but what I can do is give you the holistic tools to help you not want to drink and help you with accountability. I have had clients who went back to drinking, and I also have had clients stay sober. Here are some statistics: 80 percent of people who embark on sobriety relapse. That is with the help of AA and/or treatment centers. When it comes to this beast, no one can guarantee sobriety.

- Ask this because it will show signs that they have done the work and have healthy boundaries.

- A coach should never shell out medical advice unless they are a doctor. If they do, another red flag.

COACH TIP

I'm suggesting these at the end because I want you to ask anyone you take support from (a therapist, a sponsor or a coach) these questions. See if they have done the work. See if the therapist sees a therapist. Ask your sponsor what work they have done on themselves outside of AA. Ask them how long they have been sponsoring people in the program. Interview everyone!

Lived experience is one of the most insightful forms of knowledge you will ever receive. Gaining this from someone who has put in the put the work into themselves and is transparent about it is just pure gold.

ONLINE SUPPORT GROUPS

You can find an online support group for anything now; that is the beauty of the Internet. The COVID pandemic changed the game with virtual support and put a spotlight on these communities.

You can even find groups and programs that are specifically for you, like "sober moms," "sober dads" and "sober service industry." Seriously, there is an online support group out there for anyone.

Facebook groups alone can be extremely helpful, and they are all free. I have witnessed countless women use my Sober Vibes Facebook community as support and accountability on their sober journey. They lean into it. Recently, I had a woman post about being five years sober, and I remember the day she first started using the group for added support. In March of 2020, a woman in the Sober Vibes Facebook community started using the free meetings I was running at the time. She started at day one, but continued to use the group and just recently celebrated three years sober. I love watching these transformations and am incredibly honored to be a part of it.

Personally, I believe the best sober and recovery communities ever are on Instagram. Within these accounts, you are going to find what they offer their communities for support. Many do meetings. See what they have to offer. Find the pages you connect to and hit follow.

I would love nothing more than to recommend specific sober communities to look up, but my recommendations may not vibe with you. Also, I can't speak for creators and how long they plan on keeping communities going. Through the years, I've seen many stop talking about their sobriety because they hit so many years or got burnt out by talking about it. I totally get it! That's why I want you to go on Instagram and type in "sober" and see what comes up.

Instagram is where I hang out the most. Every Monday, I do an "ask me anything" and get to as many questions as possible, and every Saturday I do a sober check-in on my stories. Come hang and fill your social media up with awesome reminders of why alcohol is no longer for you. Online support helps, and I know many who started there and remain sober to this day because they used it as a tool.

COACH TIP

In the first thrity days of your journey, it's important to tap into a network of support in person or online, but DO NOT OVERDO IT. Recovery and sobriety burnout is real. Look at it like this: If you are trying to lose or gain weight, would you listen to 100 podcasts about it, follow 500 accounts, read 25 books and be in 50 meetings about it? Good lord, that sounds exhausting. When you start listening to 25 different people, all the information gets lost and confusing. You feel like everyone is contradicting themselves, and then at the end of the day, you have your own self and thoughts to deal with. It is a lot. As stated above, just pick a few and go from there. You can always unfollow down the road and rotate around your support.

HOMEWORK

To-Do List

☐ Do you know anyone around you who is sober? If yes, reach out and ask if you could chat. If no, look up sober accounts on Instagram and send a DM. Ask them what is one tip they have to help a person starting out on an alcohol-free journey.

☐ Add two sober accounts to your social media feeds and find one sober podcast episode to listen to each week.

What type of support do you want?

What type of support do you need?

_____

_____

_____

_____

_____

_____

_____

_____

_____

_____

_____

_____

_____

_____

_____

_____

_____

_____

_____

_____

_____

_____

_____

_____

_____

What type of support have you tried?

THE SECOND MONTH

Congratulations! You just made it thirty days without alcohol. WOOHOO. It is huge. Celebrate every day sober, but especially thirty days. It is an amazing milestone. Be proud of yourself and know I'm proud of you.

As we dig more into this section of your journey, know that this part is when you will start creating more mindset shifts and limiting beliefs when it comes to thriving in sobriety. You will be uncomfortable, and you will be shedding an old identity, but I promise you that choosing a life without alcohol will be the best decision you've ever made.

NORMALIZE LETTING GO OF ALCOHOL BECAUSE IT NO LONGER SERVES YOU.

DON'T OVERWHELM YOURSELF

Overwhelm is a dick. It's real. It's very easy in today's world to experience overwhelm on a daily basis. I still do from time to time. I don't believe overwhelm is a choice. Some will say it is, and they can go shove it where the sun don't shine. It's all about how we process things, and that's why this journey is not a one size fits all. When you never learned proper coping mechanisms, of course overwhelm is constantly going to be there. When you are quitting drinking, overwhelm can feel like it's times 100. I can't say enough how normal it is.

Yes, it's possible to not completely overwhelm yourself in this process.

Notice I said "completely." I didn't say it will never be there, because some days it will, and if you suffer from anxiety, that adds to your case.

We are human beings, and overwhelm exists, especially when we have been used to numbing out feelings and our nervous systems being in chaos for so long.

Right now, you are moving past the initial detox and starting to feel a little better. When I say "better," I mean you don't feel so shook or physically bad. "Shook" means emotionally or physically disturbed. Maybe you even experienced the opposite of being shook. Maybe you have been in the state of euphoria, often referred to as the pink cloud.

The pink cloud is a term used in recovery. If you haven't experienced it, it's okay—not everyone does. In fact, I never did. I created my own euphoria when I started exercising, eating properly and adding in the things I'm telling you about in this book.

I'm here to help you thrive in your first ninety days of sobriety realistically. I will not tell you—like so many gurus and influencers—that you MUST do twenty-five things in a day to succeed. Sometimes succeeding in a day is waking up, brushing your teeth, taking a thirty-minute walk, putting yourself back to bed and not drinking alcohol. Everyone is different and, when it comes to quitting drinking, it's not easy. Progress over perfection always.

I didn't start taking on all the things I do now at once. I didn't wake up and say I'm going to quit drinking, lose weight, be a good human, have a credit score of 800, drink 100 ounces of water a day, conquer 10,000 steps a day and solve world hunger. No thank you, sounds exhausting. I still don't achieve this on a daily basis. I don't want this for you either. Especially if it's not the speed you go at.

Taking on everything at once—I'm not a fan, because it will lead to overwhelm. Overwhelm often leads to burnouts, and then to resentments and then to relapse. As your coach, I don't want you to fall into this cycle. We want to thrive and not just continue to survive.

You will start to gain a little clarity after your first thirty days and see the world a little differently. During this time, it's still very important to continue to rest, hydrate and lean into support. Only take on so much per day; when you enter the world of sobriety and recovery, your senses become super heightened and emotions are raw. So it's very common to overstimulate yourself. Your nervous system is still healing, so dive into some self-care right now. You are still in a process you can't speed up or skip. You have to trust it and know it will get better.

I've said this before but I'm saying it again, because not a lot of people will and it's really important: Do not listen to twenty-five sober podcasts, read twenty quit-lit books, follow 100 sober accounts and go to five meetings a day. Why am I saying this? Because at the end of the day you still have your own sober self to deal with . . . your own drinking thoughts. Find a healthy balance. Life is not all about sobriety and recovery. It is not all who or what you are. Yes, it will always be a part of you, but right now, taking on other stories and perspectives can often lead to confusion and the thought of "why can't I do this!" There is a recovery burnout, and it's important to not create this overwhelm for yourself. Slow and steady. I am not saying you shouldn't dive into all the resources out there. Just find a happy balance, and allow yourself something other than just recovery in a day.

REMEMBER, ONE DAY AT A TIME

There is a principal that has been shared for decades and decades . . . and perhaps longer than that. It's a motto mostly used in the twelve-step community, but every human being should use it. It's simple yet so effective to say, "one day at a time." Pow! I hope your mind is blown and if not, that's okay too.

You have probably heard the term before, but now it will take on a whole new meaning.

When it comes to quitting drinking, there are so many future thoughts, or as I like to refer to them, future trippin'. All of a sudden, you become very thought-focused on the what ifs, the future plans and how it's going to be. You are now thinking about how it's going to be at your cousin's wedding without drinking, and the wedding is actually two years from now. Or you think about what it is going to be like going to Italy without having wine, and you haven't even booked a trip to Italy. Or "How am I going to ever have sex again without a few drinks in me?" Or "Are my friends going to like me without alcohol?"

These kinds of thoughts and more will come to mind.

Applying the one-day-at-a-time mindset eventually becomes a true state of being. When you are mindfully aware and embracing it, you worry less about future drinking situations and things you don't have control over.

Learning ODAAT very early on in my sobriety made a huge difference, and I hope it does the same for you. There will be days when it's not going to click, and you will be thinking about that non-booked trip to Italy and how it doesn't seem right to travel all the way there without drinking. Other days you will live ODAAT and have it dialed in. But don't beat yourself up if you aren't grasping it daily; it takes time and practice.

COACH TIP

Set reminders on your phone that pop up that say "One Day at a Time" at different times of the day. Morning, noon and night. Or write this motto down on sticky notes, and stick them where you can see them . . . bathroom mirror, in your car, the fridge or office.

Mindset shifts take practice, so be gentle with yourself.

WHERE THERE IS ONE . . .

Cigarettes and alcohol were my best friends.

My second vice was always cigarettes. I might have loved them more than alcohol. It's a toss-up. Let's say if the world was ending, I would go down smoking Parliament Lights. I would. I'm sharing this with you so you get the extent of how much I used to love smoking. Smoking for me started around the age of sixteen, and I quit about six weeks after I gave up drinking. When my grandmother passed away, I wrote a letter to her saying I would give up smoking when I flew back home after her funeral. I did, and my goodness, that was very hard. Talk about a complete shock to the soul. Quitting two behaviors and addictions like that. Good God.

Let me share the dates, so you see how close in time this all happened:

- August 18th: quit drinking
- September 14th: my grandma died
- September 24th ish: quit smoking

I decided to quit two addictions and lost a very important person within weeks of one another. I didn't know it at the time, but all three of these came with a grieving process. I didn't know that two vices I used as a coping mechanism would have such an effect on me. It was like losing a loved one. Looking back, I probably should have waited to quit smoking. This is where I want to help you thrive in your process. If you have a few vices, I urge you to address one vice at a time if that works best for you. I'm sure someone will read that last line and tell me that's not the move, but we have to take this at the pace that is comfy for you.

For me, quitting both vices around the same time felt like a lot of pressure. I was so emotionally charged, and some days I felt like the little girl from *The Exorcist*. I wanted to yell at random people that their mothers suck cock. I'm not kidding when I said I compared myself to a demon; it was a lot. Poor Matthew got the worst of me during those weeks.

It's no surprise that I turned to sweets and shopping that first year. I did a little transference and got my dopamine hits from sugar and swiping my credit card. It's extremely common to have two to three more addictions/ behaviors waiting around the corner for you.

I want to make something clear: I did not have a shopping or food addiction. It never got to a point where it got out of hand. I surely enjoyed the rush of buying things and eating sugar. I had a friend who went from quitting heroin to a raging drinking problem. I'm proud to say she is over six years sober. It's super common to have transference addiction, or going from one thing to the next. My therapist told me this nugget of knowledge one day while I was talking about my relationship with food. I also learned that my unhealthy relationship with food came before alcohol.

A correlation for women between eating issues and alcohol is very common. I've been told and heard you should never touch alcohol if you have issues with food. I've worked with many women whose eating issues came before the alcohol. It's wild to me that this isn't talked about more.

Above I mentioned dopamine. Dopamine is a type of neurotransmitter and hormone. It plays a role in many important body functions, including movement, memory, pleasurable reward and motivation. We as humans consistently want that feel-good feeling. It's why we might turn to things like drinking, gambling, porn, shopping and sugar.

The drinking cycle you were in has become a a reward system. You have a good day, you drink. You have a bad day, you drink. You get a promotion, you drink. You clean your house, you drink. You're throwing your child's fifth birthday party, you drink because you "deserve" it. The list goes on. Any of them ring true to you? I rewarded myself all the time, even when I shouldn't have. Makes me giggle looking back now, but that's because I can see it for what it was. You will giggle about it one day too.

To help you in this process of getting sober, if you notice some other problematic behaviors coming up right now, address them within the time you need. Right now, you should be focusing on quitting drinking. Yes, you are going to eat sweets; yes you will gain five pounds and spend extra money on fun workout clothes or another water bottle. Do not stress. Everything will even out in time. I have said to many clients that you must pick your hard right now. Little by little, it all adds up. Don't try to be the hero and say you are going do it all at once. Within three days you will have completely overwhelmed yourself and be back to day zero feeling defeated and asking yourself "why" you drank last night. There are many layers to unpack in the process of quitting drinking.

COACH TIP

Allow yourself to laugh. I know how heavy everything can feel right now, but it will not feel like this forever. One of the best tools you can use is to allow yourself the gift of laughing. If it's at your own expense or by turning something funny on. Dive into a comedy series, reality TV, a stand-up special or a funny book . . . or call a friend who makes you laugh. Laughter is the best medicine. It's helped me since day one, and I think it's one of the best ways to incorporate joy and uplift you.

Laugh every day.

I know four women who have never let me down when it comes to making me giggle with clean fun. Rose, Sophia, Blanche and Dorothy have always been my friends in this department. *The Golden Girls* never disappoint.

OVERCOMING MIND TRICKS

It wouldn't be a surprise if you told me that you have quit drinking many times and can make it to thirty to forty days before you start drinking again. I understand. When you enter the thirty- to sixty-day mark, something happens that a lot of people don't think will. A little voice inside you starts telling you that you can have one drink, and that your drinking wasn't as bad as you thought. Or, of course, you can control it—you just went thirty-something days without alcohol.

HELLO, self-sabotage!

It's crazy how we can get to a point where we know how harmful drinking alcohol is for us, take a break and then go right back to where we were before we quit. That is how quickly the addiction can escalate.

The drinker's mind will always want to drink alcohol. That is how powerful the substance is and how easily it takes over our brains.

Right now, you may even notice drinking dreams are showing up . . . dreams where you feel completely hammered and wake up in a cold sweat, having a hard time figuring out if that was real or not. Or dreams where you are so tempted you can feel the shame take over. All very common. You can't fight your subconscious. I still get drinking dreams once in a blue moon, and I'm ten years sober as I write this book. Drinking dreams come up during times of complete stress.

In March 2020, during the first couple of months after my son was born, I had a lot of drinking dreams when I did sleep. I remember these dreams now as reminders of where I never want to go back to. This is how powerful our dependency and relationship with alcohol can be. It's a spectrum of addiction.

When the thoughts come up as you continue to truck through your journey, and the voice starts saying to you that it's okay to have one drink or that you didn't have that big of a problem, my answer to you is, "The fuck you can't and the fuck you did." I say it with love. Look, you took the time to purchase this book because you know in your soul you need help, so I have to be straight with you. It will only continue to get worse and worse every time you go back to drinking, and it gets harder and harder to start over at day one. I never want to relapse because I don't have it in me to start over again. Once you get past these ninety days, you are going to feel the same way. I want you to remember that it is hard, and yes, you can do hard things. But do you want to do this over again?

Continue to connect to your "why" during moments when that little voice pops up and says you can have just one, and remember me telling you, "The fuck you can't."

COACH TIP

Anytime that voice popped up in my head telling me I could handle a drink and that it wasn't that bad, I had to say out loud, "YES, it was." I realized that I would have to acknowledge that this little voice was a real piece of work and understand it was going to be a part of me for some time. I didn't beat myself up about it. I realized the voice was part of my addiction. I had to learn to live with it, which led to more and more acceptance that I did have an issue. Within this process, I realized how much stronger of a person I was becoming when I mentally chose each day to not drink alcohol. When this happens to you, I want you to say out loud, "Yes, it was." Take some deep breaths in and then out. It's also important to understand that you are not special when it comes to being able to skip this part.

HOMEWORK

What overwhelms you when you think about not drinking in the future?

Try to write a list of 10 ideas of how you will limit overwhelm.

Do you feel like you have other addictions/impulse behaviors you need to address or work on? If so, give yourself a timeline for when you will tackle the next one.

Write out your "why" of quitting drinking. Yep, do it again.

What does "One Day at a Time" mean to you?

What type of self-sabotage behaviors come up for you?

Where did the self-sabotage start in your life? Trace it back to your childhood because, most likely, that is where this started.

Why do you think you can control your drinking?

Write down the twenty-four-hour play-by-play of what would happen if you chose to drink today.

Write some ways you will continue your self-care routine.

DESTROY THE LIMITING BELIEF THAT SOBER IS BORING.

SOBER NOT BORING

For years, while in my active addiction with alcohol, I was always the one who thought if you didn't drink you were boring. Or I wondered what people did if they didn't drink? This was my mindset, and I didn't know any better. How could I? Everyone around me drank. I worked in the service industry where drinking is a reward, and partying post shift is accepted 90 percent of the time. I grew up in a family where it was shown that drinking equals life. It surrounded me at a very early age, and I was conditioned by inner and outer influences. The culture hooked me, and I did not even ask for it.

I was an asshole who pushed booze on people. Particularly shots. Even if you didn't do shots, I made you do them. An aggressive shot pusher, I was. One time, my sister and I went to Red Lobster during the holidays after some Christmas shopping and sat at the bar. By the end of our three-hour dinner, we had that whole bar partying with shots. I'm not kidding. What was a casual seafood dinner turned into a party of people of all ages. Strangers I'd just met would soon be shot takers with me. No one asked to take shots that night; I just insisted and didn't take no for an answer. As I write this, I laugh because I think about what a menace I was. I did not care about others' boundaries; I just wanted to get wasted. Since day one, I have used humor in my life, and even in getting sober, I had to use it. This evening is one I must laugh about. Who gets people hammered at Red Lobster when all they wanted was some cheddar bays and shrimp scampi? Sissy and I did.

Also, I want you to understand this: I have never looked back at my drinking days thinking that every time I drank was god-awful. It was not. I had some fun times, and I wasn't a complete animal about 10 to 20 percent of the time I drank. I will not deny myself this. Or carry a vibe of living in continuous gloom like it was all serious. Please remember that sometimes you were just young and having fun . . . unless it was not like that for you. I don't want you to carry that gloom either. If you had some enjoyable moments, remember them. I am sure you had a ball. You can live in this space where you can feel happy in a memory that alcohol exists in and know not drinking alcohol is the best decision for you today. Because you think about alcohol, does not mean you will drink.

You may be thinking, *But I don't know anyone who doesn't drink.* I get it. I was once the girl who quit drinking at twenty-nine with zero friends and a majority of family members who drank.

The only person in my family who didn't drink was my mother, Deb, who quit in 1989, because she would get violently ill after two drinks. Deb has gone years with the question always being asked, "why don't you drink?" and people assuming she had some raging problem. Or people telling her she'd have more fun if she had a cocktail. I never recall Debbie saying to anyone that she didn't have fun. What a wild assumption to make. My mom always participated in life and had her own fun, and I give her tons of credit for it. We once did the Macarena in Miami, and Deb was stone-cold sober. She had a ball and so did my twelve-year-old self. I didn't know at the time that my mom was actually showing me you can have fun without alcohol. It wasn't until I got sober that I was able to empathize with my mother and her alcohol-free living.

EVENTUALLY, DRINKING DOES BECOME BORING

By sharing my mindset during my active relationship with alcohol, I hope to help you understand that I was one of those people who thought you couldn't have fun without alcohol. Maybe you can identify with that and see that change is possible. My mindset that sobriety was boring kept me in that relationship with alcohol longer, but again, my journey panned out how it was supposed to.

Here is a mind-blower for you (that maybe you have heard): The age you started drinking is actually the maturity level you get stuck in. Is that a fact? I don't know, but it makes a whole lot of sense. Why, after the age of thirty-five, do you care that your friends will think you are a loser because you want to quit drinking alcohol? Because your maturity level is stuck at nineteen.

If you battle with this, it is okay. I empathize because I get it, but I will share with you something my sister did with me during the height of my addiction. I was hanging out with a group that partied hard, and we had some good times, but there was a lot drinking and drug use. She told me after a heavy night of drinking, sprinkled in with some Special K, that this group of friends was not good. She went on to say—and the most important thing that stuck—if I didn't start to get my life together, I was going to wake up one day and they would all have progressed in their lives, and I would still be doing the same thing. These words hit hard because she was right and I knew it. I was probably around twenty-four or twenty-five (I can't remember the years but do know that George W. Bush was in office), and I started to get the feeling that I was going to have to give up alcohol one day. I just didn't know when and how it would happen, but in the pit of my soul, I knew it would, one day.

Kimmie was right. Those friends moved on with their lives, and to this day I don't talk to any of them.

COACH TIP

Self-care is so important right now. Self-care can consist of resting when needed, social media breaks, journaling, watching something that will make you laugh, being around supportive people and doing things that fill your cup. Do things that are going to make you feel your best during this transformative time. This isn't selfish behavior; it's healing work that is needed so you can be your best for yourself. This then ripples into your family, relationships and work. Everyone benefits from you taking care of you. Put your oxygen mask on first.

HOBBIES

Are you wondering, *how then do I make my sobriety fun?* I have some solutions for you, but first I want to share a funny story.

Within the first sixty days, I realized quickly that I had zero hobbies. All I did was work—a very aggressive amount for a very long time because I have supported myself since I was eighteen. I conditioned myself to work doubles, pick up shifts on days off and always have more than one stream of income while working two or three jobs. When you don't have financial support from your parents early on, you condition yourself for financial survival. And let me add here that if no one explains to you finances, budgeting, investing and how money works, you of course have to work a shit-ton. With my work always being number one, it really doesn't leave much room to enjoy life. And working in the service industry comes with the culture of drinking and partying. Since my relationship with alcohol started at nineteen, and my work ethic developed earlier, this cycle was very impressionable on me. You think self-care and finding joy was discussed twenty years ago? Hell no. However, sidenote: My self-care was the church of the cinema. Going to see movies was always, and always will be, one of the loves of my life.

Now that you have my backstory of me doing nothing but working since I was eighteen, it's time to share the funny story. I will never forget sitting on the couch a few weeks after getting sober, Googling hobbies. Yes, you read that correctly. Have a laugh; you must think it's funny. I read about twenty-five things you could do, and my mind was blown. Some of these things I actually did at one point of my life. You know baking is a hobby? Reading books, writing, riding bikes and arts and crafts? All hobbies. Shit, even riding horses could be a hobby.

I remember Matthew coming home during my Google search and asking me what I was doing. I simply said, "Googling hobbies." The man was caught off guard and said, "You serious?" Yes, I was, and we laughed. In typical Matthew fashion, he helped me find something to fill my time and stay busy. We settled on some craft, and thank goodness my main squeeze is extremely talented. A real artist he is, but he will never admit it. So, he explained to me about Mod Podging, which is decoupage. Pretty much, I glued photos from books we had in our home that had pinup girls and started using these pages to decoupage picture frames and furniture. I dug it. I felt creative and accomplished. I became a crafter! It was the start of finding things to get curious about, creating and doing something other than drinking.

For about three to four months, I decoupaged my way through days, nights and my witching hours. I sat and focused on something outside of myself and booze. At this time, we had just gotten Netflix, and I needed a wholesome show. I quickly realized that drinking in the reality shows I used to watch was one way of triggering and jarring my nervous system. I settled on *Friday Night Lights* and binged all five seasons. I sat still and pushed through those early days. What I didn't do in the first few months of sobriety was to continue to move and shake like I had in my active addiction. I was not concerned during those days how this would affect my social life. I had to finally say enough to the thoughts of "losing friends" or "what will they think?" It didn't matter anymore, because at the end of the day, my wellbeing was more important than the social scene. I chose me. I had to sit in the space of One Day at a Time. I started my own day-to-day routine: work, come home to craft, watch Coach Taylor and the football team in West Texas and go to bed. Repeat. I continued to not drink and made a ridiculous amount of decoupage picture frames. I was fully embracing Coach Taylor's mantra, "Clear eyes, full hearts, can't lose."

I also started baking again. It was a love of mine when I was a kid. So yes, I guess I did have some hobbies at one point of my life.

My parents split when I was seven. So, I spent the weekends at my dad's, and he would let me choose a boxed cake, cookies or brownies mix that I could make on my own. I loved it and took a lot of pride in making something and sharing it with my siblings and father. It was fun and a great memory. So, early in my sobriety, I turned back to baking. The same feelings came back to me. I felt creative, I got lost in time and I enjoyed giving my baked goods to people. During the holidays, I started my own tradition of baking for friends and family.

Crafting made me feel good! Giving cookies away at Chirstmas made me feel good! Watching a family high school drama made me feel good!

It's crucial you do things right now that make you feel good. This is the vibe.

When you get sober, the amount of time you have on your hands is crazy, and you have no clue what to do with it. Funny how in your relationship with alcohol, you feel like you have time for nothing. Once you get sober, you actually see how much time you spent drinking. I've spent hundreds of hours sitting at bars. Hundreds. That is only the amount of time spent on the act of drinking. You also spend time thinking about alcohol pre and post the act of drinking. Thoughts of drinking prevent you from living in the present because you are itching for the time you can start drinking. There are the hours spent drinking alcohol; putting limitations on how many drinks you can have so you can function in the morning; sleeping well, which isn't happening now; waking up hungover and then feeling anxious as the cycle starts all over again.

I worked with a client who made a chart and mapped out the twenty-four hours of his drinking cycle. When you see something like that, it does wake you up and force you to ask, *Is this what I want to focus a majority of my time on?*

You are more in a cycle than you know right now, and with clarity, you will see it in a different light and how exhausting it is.

Now that you have all this time on your hands, it's time for you to find a hobby and start getting curious about something other than booze.

The number-one way to find a hobby, besides Googling it like I did, is to revisit when you were a kid. What did you enjoy doing? Let the inner child out! Go back to when you did not feel the way you do now towards people, places and things. Did you like reading? Writing? Bike riding? Did you color or paint? Did you used to play an instrument or were you the kid who tried out for all the plays because you loved acting? Did you enjoy dance? Were you a crafter or baker? The inner child in you did something and loved it. Find that kid, go back and remember.

If by some chance nothing is sparking joy from hobbies from your childhood, here is another way to find something:

What is something you have always wanted to learn to do in your adult life but haven't gotten to yet because you know you "never had time," or, if you were like me, the booze kept you in your little bubble? Maybe you have always wanted to be a yogi, or you always wanted to volunteer and help at food banks or hang with the elderly. Volunteering and donating your time are hobbies.

The sky is the limit when it comes to what you can do and learn.

All of these hobbies are putting you in a different state of being and doing than you have been in for years. I challenge you to start now. I'm not saying overload your life and think you HAVE to do all the things. Remember, I don't believe in that. I do believe in picking one hobby and kicking ass with it. Enjoy it, be kid-like and connect with something outside of your drinking self. If you don't end up enjoying the hobby, pick another one.

You might have heard that the disease of addiction is a thinking disease. It is true. You think, you think some more and you will continue to think for future years to come if you allow yourself. Finding a hobby gives you the ability to not be so inside your brain. Your mind actually goes quiet when you are in the act of learning, creating or giving back. It's five stars.

COACH TIP

Start doing your new hobby during your witching hour, the time you would usually start to drink. I would get myself all lined-up on Friday nights (towards the end of my drinking career that was *the* night) with snacks, decoupage and *Friday Night Lights* around 6:30 p.m. All of a sudden, it was 10 o'clock and time for bed, and I made it without alcohol. Time flies when you are having good, clean fun. Some of those Fridays, I would bake, and then get into crafting. A double-feature of creating.

FUN TIMES

I already know your question. Trust me, I won't have you locked up in the house coloring adult coloring books and binge-watching wholesome TV. You are probably thinking, *Well, okay, I do that, but what about my social life?* We'll get into that in the next chapter. Here, I'm going to give you a list of ideas of things to do and ways to get out of your house, because I know this feels lonely and you want some excitement: concerts, museums, sporting events, plays, movies, cooking classes, dining out and spending time in nature hugging a tree or two.

I also have a free Sober Not Boring calendar you can download at my website www.courtneyrecovered.com. The calendar gives you something to do for thirty days. All my resources are also provided in the back of this book.

Perhaps you did some of the activities listed above during your drinking days or maybe you did not. I can assure you the association of these events and drinking go hand-in-hand, but they don't have to in this new life. I had anxiety during my first sober concert, which I had to keep working through the first hour there. Deep breathing and repeating to myself, "I am exactly where I need to be right now," helped. As the night went on and I got more comfortable being there and started enjoying the show, the anxiety lessened. By the end of it, I had actually enjoyed my overall experience and was incredibly proud of myself for attending my first concert without booze since my mother forced me to go see Brooks & Dunn in the seventh grade because my brother was a fan.

In my sobriety, I started exploring more things to do, and museums and exhibits became a big one for me. Do you know you could spend about four hours in a museum, reading and taking in the all history? Get lost in time and the beauty of art all without alcohol. Yes, I know you can buy alcohol at many of these things, but it doesn't mean you have to. I get it, but alcohol is not the main focus. Alcohol helps make businesses money, so if they can have it there they will. It's the world we live in, and not everyone who drinks has a problem. I accepted that fact within this timeframe on my sober journey and saw it for what it was. I have to be blunt with you: You have to get super uncomfortable some days to be comfortable in a world full of alcohol. You might have to work through the discomfort of walking by someone carrying a drink in their hand or waiting in line for a soda pop and the person in front of you is getting a glass of wine. I'm sure this isn't something you wanted to hear, but it's the truth, and it's important to keep reminding yourself why you are better off without alcohol. In time it will not bother you, but right now it will.

COACH TIP

When it comes to going out and participating and seeing people drink, you will have your feelings about it. You will get super-jealous and angry some days, wondering why you can't just be a normal drinker or why you can't moderate. Listen, moderation is what normal drinkers do. I want you to understand your brain is different than others' and that is okay. You are not a freak. You are just part of a club of millions. Your motto is—which I hope you accept—"It's okay that they drink; I won't because I am better off without alcohol." Empower your little sober ass with the way you see things and how yo talk to yourself. It works.

MINDSET

According to Google, "mindset" is defined as the established set of attitudes held by someone. Look, Google and I are besties. If I don't know, I look it up.

When you quit drinking and start living a sober life, you have to do a lot of self-awareness, reflecting and attitude changing. You can see the world differently if you choose.

I say "choose" here because some people get sober and still live in doom and gloom. They like it. They like self-pity and victimization, but there are people out there who don't have drinking problems who also live like this. It's all up to the person. I am a believer that happiness is an attitude and a mindset.

The mindset shift here is crucial for living the sober life you want. I am not throwing toxic positivity at you here either. I know how hard life has been for a lot of people, and I do not deny your feelings. You can feel that and you should, but also learning about mindset helps you understand there are ways to live and choose a happier state of mind. Sober life isn't a punishment. You, my friend, get to live two lives in one. The life in active addiction and now this sober life. Not many get to see life this way.

Here is an awesome mindset shift to remember. How much fun did you really have during your active relationship with alcohol? Maybe an hour, if that? Is waking up hungover, lying on the couch the next day fun? Is having hangover anxiety or panic attacks the next day fun? Is browning out or blacking out fun? Is having health issues due to drinking fun? Is looking at your kids the next day and wondering what you said the night before fun? Is living the same cycle every three months fun?

Absolutely not.

So how much fun is drinking really? It is not all that great, especially when you have a problem with it. That's why you have to shift this mindset around and step out of the façade. With time your clarity will continue to show you what a delusion you were living in. I'm not shaming here but giving you tough, sober love.

Before I end this chapter, I want to add something extremely important. Many people think sober is boring or that living in sobriety gives one that bored or even lonely feeling. This is a you problem. You feel bored because you aren't living in chaos. You might have been born into chaos and this is all you know. So when you quit drinking and start doing work on yourself like you are doing in this book, the cycle of chaos starts becoming less. You don't know how you feel about it because the comfortable feeling of chasing chaos is now the uncomfortable feeling of living in sobriety. There are no messes to clean up, apology tours to go on and (my favorite) your actions no longer make you feel like an asshole. The boredom can kick in because you and your nervous system do not quite yet know how to sit in this feeling. Let yourself be bored; being bored is not a bad thing in life. That is why it's important to figure out something to do with your time. Remember, chaos is not cool, and you deserve a life now without it.

If you feel lonely, examine the feeling. Is this more of an internal or external feeling? If you do have friends, family, a partner and an animal, then it's more of an internal feeling. I want you to give yourself some time to work on this. You could have been feeling lonely for years, and a reason why you drank was to cover up this inner feeling. You will have to figure out why you have always felt like this. If you feel lonely because you do not have friends, family and/or a partner, why is this? Have you isolated yourself? Have you never liked people? Have you tried making friends? I will share that both these external and internal feelings of loneliness are going to take some time and work. Don't give up on it or make an excuse to keep drinking because it fills this void. The healing started the day you stopped drinking. All of it is figureoutable.

COACH TIP

Connect to one of your worst hangovers/fallouts from alcohol you have ever had. Hold that memory close, feel it, taste the hangover in your mouth, feel the shame of it. Connect on a daily basis if need be. I always allow myself to connect with my drinking self on Sundays. I remembered this so I could be reminded of how life used to be. I didn't shame myself for it, but instead, I allowed the memories and feelings to come back, and I sat in it for a few minutes. I thanked the universe I wasn't there in present day. Remembering where alcohol took you is always a great reminder of where you do not want to be anymore. Remember the pain alcohol has caused you.

HOMEWORK

Why did you decide to quit drinking? Yes, write it out again.

What hobbies were you into as a kid?

Describe three things you have always wanted to learn to do as an adult but never did because drinking never allowed you to.

Write out your twenty-four-hour drinking cycle. How much time really went into your cycle?

What can you do today to brighten someone else's day? Buy a stranger a coffee, send a nice text to your mother asking how she is doing, make dinner for your partner? Write out five ideas.

What fun activities can you do in your area? Write out things to do.

Sober Not Boring

What current mindset do you have around quitting drinking alcohol? Are you mad, excited, ready, determined to never go back to where you once were?

Have you always lived in chaos? If so, write down some examples from your life.

What about chaos is so comfortable for you?

Write about one of your worst hangovers with alcohol.

YOU WILL CHANGE FOR THE BETTER WHEN YOU QUIT DRINKING ALCOHOL.

BUILDING NEW ROUTINES

Structure is about to be your best friend. You may be thinking, *I am already structured. I get up, get ready, go to work, do the things needed in a day and then go to sleep.* Yes, I'm sure that's how your day is, BUT there are always ways to tweak your schedule, so you run your day instead of your day running you. The compound of chaos can bleed into your day-to-day. I do not doubt it. In fact, I'm sure you didn't realize how much it did. It's crucial around this time to start building new routines and structure for yourself. It's totally fine to not focus on this for those first thirty days when you are just focused on not drinking. We are going to start adding to your day.

Adding routine will help you out more than you know, and time will continue to tell you how important it is. Routines create a feeling of good. You end up setting a tone for each and every day that helps you control you. Setting the tone for the day could also be the difference between relapsing or not. It does not feel good to wake up late, rush, run out the door with nothing to eat and then suddenly get hit with the day from hell and you have zero control of it. You come home, and because you had such a shit day, you drink wine because *Why not? My day didn't go as planned.* Sound familiar?

You carry the control of YOU, and I am a firm believer that setting yourself up in your habits starts in the morning. I cannot say it enough: *You set the tone.* You will continue to thrive in your sober journey when you incorporate what I'm sharing with you.

BREAKING OLD CYCLES

Here's an example of a daily routine of the old drinking you:

Wake up the very last possible minute because I'm sure you weren't feeling all that great from the night before. Maybe you showered, maybe you didn't, but I'm sure you were rushing out the door with coffee and some type of carbohydrate to soak up the alcohol and try to make you feel better.

You proceed with your day feeling not so good, annoyed with work and family, and then 2:00 p.m. nears and you start thinking about the next drink. You think of what to drink, where and the time you will start drinking. The paranoia—with a dash of alcohol detox sweats—probably creeps in as you wonder if anyone has caught on to your issue with booze. You may even start thinking about making stops at different bars and even the liquor store. Mentally, this is when you check-out at work or with the kids because now you are just hyper-focused on the next drink. You leave your day and rush to get to your destination of choice where you start to do your drinking. You are immediately relieved once alcohol hits your lips because you have stopped the withdrawals, and you are in what you think is your happy place where all is right and you can completely numb out whatever you are escaping, be it thoughts, feelings or the Groundhog Day you think is your life.

After you settle into your drinking space, you then start telling yourself how much you will have to drink and what time you will go to sleep because you don't want to feel tomorrow how you did today. You drink past the time and amount you said you would. You numb out for a few hours, and then go to sleep without brushing your teeth or washing your face. (Maybe you did this. One of my besties always washed up hammered. Even Stevie Nicks said she always washed her face at night, even in high partying days. So maybe you got this down. I never did. I would wake up the next day looking like Alice Cooper, you know, with the mascara running down my face.) Okay, back to your routine . . . you miss out on another night being present with your kids, being productive or maybe even a present partner. Or you cry yourself to sleep in a drunken rage because you feel so alone. You sleep terribly because, scientifically, you do not get a good night sleep when drinking and you wake up the next morning and start your day over just the like one before and before that one and so on.

This cycle is the pits.

I know I used an example of someone having a 9 to 5 job as part of someone's day. This sort of routine is also for stay-at-home moms or dads, part-timers, night-shifters and retirees. Apply it to your life however your day looks; I am sure it's very similar to how you did your day.

What I have described for you is an unhealthy cycle that has become your routine. It's almost like you are on autopilot.

In your new sober skin, it's crucial to start creating a new healthy daily routine. One that feels good to you. One that will not make you feel like you're still in the active relationship with alcohol simply minus the alcohol. Yes, this is real, and I talk about it in the next section (page 123).

In the Sober Not Boring chapter, I talked about finding things to do with hobbies and activities (page 101). In this chapter, you will incorporate these in your new daily routine. That's why you need to replace an old hobby with a new healthy one. Instead of coming home from work and sitting in your chair in the garage or living room, come home, tie up your laces and go for an hour walk. You come home and call someone who you enjoy talking to. You come home and make yourself a cup of tea and start coloring in your adult coloring book. You come home and presently engage with your children. If home is a trigger, you can always go straight to a gym, yoga class, mediation studio, art studio, museum and/or a meeting. You have options.

The words "I have nothing to do" should never come out of your mouth, and I know it will feel like that in these early days, but the world is your oyster, and there are tons of things to do, learn and see.

COACH TIP

Wake up at the same time every morning and try to go to bed at the same time every night. Even on the weekends, if you can, just for a little bit. Doing this is going to start your new healthy sleep routine. Sleep is crucial when it comes to healing the body and having your body functioning properly. Alcohol impacts sleep systems in your body in these ways: it decreases melatonin, reduces growth hormones, increases stress hormones, aggravates breathing problems and disrupts your circadian rhythm.

I know when I go to bed super-late, past midnight, I am a wreck the next day. I feel hungover, eat shitty and feel tired all day long. I was a person who used to always stay up until 3:00 or 4:00 a.m., but when I got sober, I worked extremely hard on fixing my sleep. It's possible. Another good thing to do when you wake up is to get some sunlight on your face. This will help your body's circadian rhythm. Be consistent with it, and in time, you will start feeling a lot better than you are right now.

DAILY STRUCTURE

Structure is key.

Having structure in your life will make you feel sane! I am serious. It is going to feel extremely uncomfortable when you start. The uncomfortableness is because this is new. You are stepping outside and breaking years of patterns. Many of us saw the same patterns from our parents, so we are then also breaking generational cycles here. Give yourself a *Fuck yes, I am doing this thing.*

Structure is adding a pattern or organization to your day. When it comes to your daily structure, you must create what this looks like for yourself. What I have learned with creating structure and routine for the early days of sober living and beyond is that it makes you feel good.

You are getting into a new way of living, a new groove, if you will, which will help you when it comes to long term sobriety. When you create structure for yourself in your daily routine, you are starting to silence the long-term chaos you were used to. When you create this new pattern and live it every day, you are no longer welcoming in the chaos but instead rewiring your brain and making new patterns for yourself.

When I got sober, I continued to live like I was in my active addiction—living in a stuck state of mental chaos like I was nineteen. Waking up at the very last minute, letting the tone of the day be determined by my continued last-minute chaos, rushing to work giving myself unnecessary anxiety and just not being organized in my life, even with how my closet was arranged. Shit was everywhere in the sense that all areas of my life needed some TLC.

I believe my shift was probably about six months in. I woke up one day and was just fed up with feeling like chaos was still existing in my life even though I gave up booze.

There comes a point in sobriety when you hit this wall. Like, *Okay, I gave up drinking but why do I still feel this way?* It's because there is work that needs to be done. Like the homework I'm making you do (that you are doing, right?). The compound effect is real, but you will still have some cleaning up from who you were and what you did during your active relationship with alcohol. Everything doesn't disappear at last sip, but it is a start. You must then start working on your emotional sobriety after you feel secure in yourself not physically drinking. I know it seems like a lot, but remember, little by little it all adds up.

When I started creating structure for myself, it was my next step in the process. The simple step I started working towards was waking up at the same time each morning and going to bed the same time every night. Also, I gave myself time in the morning by not hitting the snooze button thirty-five times to the point where I was rushing out the door speeding down the road stressing out my nervous system and looking like a maniac. Are you picking up what I'm laying down? I know you feel me on this.

Creating structure is going to take time, so don't ever feel like you failed if one day you kill the game and the next day you completely revert back to before. Progress not perfection. You are totally reprogramming yourself here, so be gentle on your soul and do the best you can each day.

COACH TIP

The best way to start adding structure to your day is to buy a calendar or use one on your phone. Schedule your day! Even schedule your day off! If you plan to binge-watch a series, write it down. That way your "free time" never feels like it needs to go to drinking alcohol when you already have a plan. When you write it down, you are ten times more likely to do it.

MORNING AND NIGHT ROUTINES

A perfect way to start creating your daily structure is getting into a morning and night routine. Look at this as your foundation for the day. You get to set the tone for your day, and the only person who has control over this is you.

Before giving you suggestions about morning and night routines, please remember that you do not need to do this all at once. Take your time to stack these rituals and routines. When I say stack, pick one to two, get into the rhythm of creating this new habit and then add something else to the routine. Do not pick ten things to do and by day four, you say this is too much and feel overwhelmed and defeated.

Your morning routine is you setting the tone for the day. You create the energy. You create the vibe. YOU CREATE. See how much power you actually have.

I will share with you my morning routine pre and post having a child. I'm not so far away from how life was like before my son. I still remember.

Pre Child

- Wake up between 6:30 and 7:00 a.m.
- Make bed
- Drink water with salt/daily green juice
- Coffee
- Meditation
- 10-25 minutes of reading a personal development book
- Gratitude journal: 4 things I'm grateful for
- Exercise 3 to 5 days a week
- Get on with my day

Post Child (5 months to 14 months)

- Wake up between 5:30 and 6:15 a.m.
- Make bed
- Get baby. Feed him.
- Water with salt/daily green juice
- Coffee
- 10-20 minutes of reading
- Gratitude journal: 4 things I'm grateful for
- Get on with my day

I know people get hung up on morning routines because they think they need to be doing hours of stuff, and that is simply not the case. You can if you want, but I wanted to clear it up and show you something realistic.

My morning routine has become one of my greatest tools in my recovery. It's where I connect to be centered. Yes, making my bed, drinking coffee (which, fun fact, I didn't start drinking until I got sober, and now I look forward to my morning coffee before I go to bed the night before), reading a personal development book, meditating and writing out what I'm grateful for. It's daily me time. Which we all need.

Even on vacations I connect and center. This routine really is nonnegotiable. Of course, there have been some mornings where my routine got thrown off due to things out of my control, like being sick, having a migraine or traveling super early. But I always pick up where I left off when the next day presents itself. If for some reason I go more than a few days without doing my morning routine, I then move the reading and gratitude journal to nighttime. As you see, post-child, meditation is not included because I had to switch this to nighttime.

What you will also notice is I DO NOT TOUCH MY phone. I used to allow all the notifications and other people's energy into my head and soul at 6:30 a.m. It's a terrible way to start the day. Seriously. You do not need to take it on so early. Do you first. Set limits and boundaries with the phone. I once heard motivational speaker Mel Robbins ask, "Would you allow 300 people in your bedroom? So, why are you doing it with your phone?" I felt that one because she is not wrong. Have you ever opened a disappointing email at 6:30 in the morning? It sets the tone for the day, and the anxiety kicks in before you even had your morning pee. But if you waited and did you first, you could have felt that 10:00 a.m. differently. By not letting these energies in so early, you can protect your mental health.

Your nighttime routine is equally as important and it sets you up for the next day. My nights have become a different type of me time, and one I look forward to. What does your nighttime routine look like? Do you have one? If you don't, it's time to get yourself settled into one. Again, you don't need to be doing 1,000 things at night to create a nighttime routine. But give yourself something to decompress from the day and create a serene atmosphere for yourself.

Here is what my nighttime looked like pre- and post-child

Pre Child

- Clean kitchen
- Wash up/jammies
- Light an incense
- My stories . . . aka Bravo shows
- Sleep

Post Child

- Clean kitchen
- Shower/jammies
- Light an incense
- Nighttime tea
- My stories . . . aka Bravo shows
- Meditation
- Sleep

The nighttime pre- and post-child are very similar besides me switching my mediation around. Trying to do my meditation in the morning with a baby no longer worked. So, I had to adjust and found that meditation before bed became extremely helpful on so many levels. It chilled me out and decompressed me in a healthy way as a first-time mother. That's also why I switched my showers to nighttime. Talk about an energy release from the day!

I also don't allow myself to turn on the television during the day. Once I start, I will not stop. We can laugh at that comment and my true addict brain. It is something that took me a long time to realize in my sobriety. It didn't make me feel good to piss away a day and not get XYZ done because I binged a season of *Vanderpump Rules*. So, I made a deal with myself to wait until nighttime for TV. Yes, of course if I'm sick or if my son is napping and I need a mommy mental break, it gets turned on. But there are tiny exceptions to my boundaries. I'm not a total anal freakshow. I allow a balance.

I'm also not going to tell you to go without TV or say it's a way of numbing out.

Yes, of course if your intention is to use it in that way then it's an issue. Allow yourself some joy, and if your stories bring it to you, then more power to you. Nowadays, some of these gurus are getting too extreme, and it's so easy for you to be asking yourself in your sober path if you're doing this right. You might have read on an Instagram post you should be doing 101 things that don't include watching *Real Housewives*. If your stories bring you joy, continue.

Create a nighttime routine that will work best for you!

For further help, you can download a free PDF called Sober Routine Workbook. Check out the resource page (page 192) for this. The workbook has ideas for both morning and night, along with a printable daily checklist. Use it to help you with creating your new sober routine.

COACH TIP

When assessing your morning and nighttime routine, start with the night first. What are a few things you can do at night to set up your morning for success? What is important to you? Is waking up to a clean kitchen going to make you feel good? Does packing your lunch at night make the most amount of sense, so you don't have to rush with the kids in the morning? Is making an 8:00 p.m. in-person or virtual meeting going to continue to keep your sobriety moving forward? Get organized with this and write it out; that way it might not feel so overwhelming.

I used to have this weird thing with time, and I would think that doing something would take longer than it did. And this mindset then had me not do that something because I thought it would take hours—this included my night routine. I learned if I just did it and followed through, the time was a lot shorter. And I felt amazing after it was done. For example, cleaning the kitchen each night so my next morning was chaos free and I didn't have to add something to my list like cleaning all the dishes in the sink.

Just do it.

REMEMBER, THIS FEELS GOOD

What is the point of creating routine and structure in your day in sober life?

Easy. It's extremely important for you to feel good each and every day. I have said a few times in this chapter you should do things that are going to make you feel good. The better you feel, the easier it will get for you to not want to drink. Therefore, creating routines and structure is key for a successful, sober you.

Using the beauty products you spent hundreds of dollars on that are sitting underneath your bathroom sink right now will make you feel good. Will they solve your internal problems? Absolutely not, but it's a start.

Creating routine and new habits is being the sober person you have wanted for yourself. Remember how I said that even though I was sober, I still felt like I was living in my active addiction? Well, that's because the only thing that changed for me that first year was the fact that I quit the act of drinking. My actions and day-to-day living did not match my new sober self. Lots of layers.

The sooner you start creating your structure during this time between thirty and sixty days, the better off you will be.

Keep doing the things that make you feel good. No, drinking alcohol does not make you feel good in the long run. So flick that thought out of your mind.

COACH TIP

You do not need to go out and buy 101 things that you think might make you feel better right now. I want you to go through your home and see what you have bought in your active drinking days that you haven't used yet. Is it maybe all the facial products? Maybe even some clothes you haven't worn yet? Ten unused cute journals? Some Epsom salt for taking baths? Fifty candles you have not used? I am sure there is something around your home right now that you can start using to make yourself feel better and incorporate with your new routine.

HOMEWORK

How do you want to show up in your life every day?

How will you create a healthy sleep routine?

**What does your morning and night routine look like now?
Describe them.**

What do you want your morning and night routine to look like in your sober life?

Write out your new morning routine.

Write out your new night routine.

What are you going to do for yourself to make you feel good each day?

THE THIRD MONTH

I am proud of you for coming this far. Congratulations on making it to today. I know this work is not easy, and showing up sober each day can be challenging, but remember you are doing this for a better you and the life you want. You deserve to feel good each day, have success, feel loved and be alive today. I am always cheering you on.

IT'S EASY TO FEEL BORED IN SOBER LIFE BECAUSE, FOR ONCE IN A VERY LONG TIME, YOU ARE NOT LIVING IN CHAOS.

GRIEVING YOUR OLD DRINKING SELF

Never in a million years did I think I would go through a grieving process when it came to quitting drinking. It might sound silly, but I promise you, you will go through it too.

Around the three-month mark of sobriety, you may notice some feelings coming up and wonder why. You may have even noticed some tears. I will tell you I cried my entire first year of sobriety. I suggest a shower cry. They are amazing.

Do not be afraid of these feelings. It's okay to feel. You might have been told to suppress your feelings before your drinking problem by a parent, or that your feelings didn't matter. My suggestion is to embrace them, deal with them in baby steps and again, cry it out.

Even if feelings have not hit you yet, they will. It is quite possible you could still be on the pink cloud if you are one who has been experiencing the euphoria since you quit drinking, but those fluffy pink clouds will crash, and you will be faced with these feelings. You can always reread this section if this happens to you so you understand how to process the emotions you are going through.

Grief waits for no one and will come one day.

UNDERSTANDING THE GRIEVING PROCESS

The grieving process is a whirlwind that hits you in a sequence of emotions over a period.

What is the grieving process? I will share the stages of grief below and relate it to a person who has quit drinking.

Grief: It is time to give up drinking and instantly there is a LOSS that feels like a death.

Denial: You can't believe this is happening. How did you get here; why can't you be a normal drinker? Some jealousy will also arise with denial. For example, you get jealous that other people can be normal drinkers and you cannot just have one.

Anger: You suddenly are getting pissed at slogans you see at stores saying "it's wine o'clock," "trust me you can dance—vodka," "let's drink about it," "mommy juice," "I'm the fun mom" and so on. You also find yourself seething at Corona beer ads on TV. You are starting to hate your partner because they are going out for beers with friends. Then the inner rage towards Big Alcohol starts to take over.

Depression: The sadness starts. You find yourself crying for no reason. The heaviness weighs on your chest, and sometimes it's hard getting out of bed. You can't put your finger on the feeling, but you've got the blues. Within the sadness of it, the "loneliness" comes to the forefront.

Bargaining: You find thoughts coming to mind out of the blue like, *I didn't have that bad of a problem, I didn't have any rock bottoms, I functioned, I can just have one, maybe I just drink on special occasions* and *I'm alone, no one will know if I have a few.*

Acceptance: You realize an alcohol free life is the new normal for you and you accept that others can drink alcohol but you are a person who doesn't want it in your life, because you are so much better without it.

Are you currently in any of these stages? I can't state it enough that it is completely normal if you are in any of these stages of grief with alcohol. It is not stupid, and don't beat yourself up thinking you should be able to handle your feelings better. You are human. Be human. Humans feel and grow attachments and are flawed. This does not make you weak. Understanding this process will only help you out in the long run.

COACH TIP

Ride out the emotions of the grieving process. If you need an ugly cry in the shower or a rage scream in your car, do it. The more you let these emotions out in a healthy way, the better you will feel. How to deal with emotions now that you are sober? Journal, talk them out with a therapist, color, paint, share if you're in a support group and, my favorite, work it out with exercise. Anger and a kickboxing/boxing class equal delight. What matters is that you understand that emotions are energy. And releasing that energy in a positive way is getting it out of your being and not holding onto it.

YES, YOU HAD A RELATIONSHIP WITH ALCOHOL

It is true. You did. Accept it. Alcohol became your best friend.

I have always described my relationship with alcohol as a toxic one. With that said, I need to clear something up. Describing a relationship with a substance is not the same as admitting you are an alcoholic. (If you're not down with labels, then at least admit you are on the spectrum of alcohol use disorder or that you know you have a problem with alcohol. I'm not here to tell you how to identify, and I always state that with clients, but I do need you to admit and understand that there is an issue.)

There is no shame in the admitting game.

Right now, I want you to think about your daily routine with alcohol when you were an active drinker. How many times you thought about it. How many times you partied with it. How many times you put so much thought into it making you feel better. The love/hate you had with it . . . the I-am-never-going-to-drink-you-again-because-I-just-feel-bad-with-you day-after motto. How much energy was spent overall with alcohol. It was a lot.

Now I want you to compare this to a relationship with a person you had in your life. Friend or partner. We have all had that one relationship where we were in a vicious, toxic cycle. We knew they were no good for us, but we kept going back until we had to sever the ties completely. Once we got some distance and time from that person, we could see how much better off we were without them. This is no different with alcohol.

You may have been in this type of relationship with alcohol for years, and you kept asking yourself when it was going to end. Well, the time is now, and the only one changing the dynamics with it is you. It is time to break up with alcohol for good.

COACH TIP

No matter how intoxicating the relationship was with alcohol, it's important for you to know that you are better off without it. That going back means you are just going to end up where you left off. I want you to keep empowering yourself during this time, and remember you are deserving of so many good things. This mantra helps, use it: "I deserve to be happy and free."

When you gain some clarity in your sobriety, you will see how free you become when you are no longer in the cycle. Keep repeating the mantra above as needed and especially for anytime the voice in your head starts to tell you that you can have just one drink.

LETTING GO OF THE LAST RELATIONSHIP

So how do you let go of the relationship with alcohol? Time. Choosing every day to not engage with it. Allowing yourself to feel the feelings and having grace with yourself.

The transition you are currently in takes time, and as silly as it may now seem, it's the way to go. You may even be thinking, *I cannot believe this is what this feels like: a bad breakup.* But that is exactly what it is.

The comfort you found in alcohol is unlike any other. The only people who understand this type of comfort are those who loved it just as much as you did. That is why community will always be key here. Talking about it with others who understand helps. Matthew never got it when I tried explaining my relationship with alcohol, and I found myself feeling resentful towards him. But in all honesty, how could he have gotten it? He never had a problem, he hated alcohol. Me? I loved it. So go easy on the people around you if you find yourself getting irritated that they don't relate to the same toxic love affair you had with alcohol.

Letting go of alcohol means you physically stop going back to it. You stop telling yourself it will get better and you have control over it. You cut ties completely. You take the see-you-later, middle-finger approach. Shout *adios*, bye-bye loser from the rooftops. Continue to remind yourself how much better off you are with alcohol no longer in your life.

You play the twenty-four-hour tape in your head of what will happen if you decide to pick up alcohol and take the first sip. Where is drinking alcohol going to lead you tomorrow? Will you feel worse about yourself? It's kinda like if you went back to that partner you had sex with but then they ghosted you . . . again. Is that moment/encounter worth the fallout? The answer is NO because, at this point in your relationship with alcohol, it is never going to get better. You will never feel the butterflies in your stomach like you once had. The excitement and euphoria around it are no longer there.

But no one just cuts it out once and never goes back. This is usually a process. For some people, it takes a few times or years for them to get their hand burned so bad on the stove that they realize, okay I am done and not going back.

It did for me; four years my friend . . . four years. I tried all the ways to make this relationship work until I surrendered to the fact it was not meant to be, and that was okay.

Time will show you how much better off you are without alcohol.

In the process of letting go of the relationship with alcohol, there is something else you must start letting go of, and that is the person you once were. Oh, yes. You are going to grieve the drink, and then your old drinking self. I am sure you didn't want to hear this; no one usually does.

You might have been that "party person" in your group of friends and family. That is the type of identity and role you took on. Maybe that was just given to you or you actually gave it to yourself. You were the fun person, the one who would get people up dancing, the life of the party, the wild one, the crazy one, the one who lived in their glory days and the one that got people out of their shells. I was that person.

If this was also you and who you were in the circle you rolled with, it's okay. You may even feel like for years you had to keep this role going because you sensed people only liked you for this reason. You continued to play this role, and you were slowly dying inside while going home at 1:00 a.m. in a blackout, ugly crying and wishing it would end.

You have so much more to offer people than the party person you once were. People love you for you! Not the energy you bring because your state is induced by alcohol.

With letting go of this old identity, which is what it was, you will transition and gain a new one of who you are today. Letting go of your old drinking self means so much. Maybe there were old traits besides the relationship with alcohol you had that you want to free yourself of. Like lying, being a procrastinator, having a limitless mindset and so on. You can shed this old self and rebuild a new sober you.

In the process of letting your old self go, there will come healing, growth and an allowing for the time to guide you. You can't rush it, so don't even try.

COACH TIP

Shifting and becoming a newer, better version of yourself are good things and all happen in the timeframe they are supposed to. Embrace this shift. Look at it as a positive. Releasing and letting go of things that no longer serve you is empowering. You may lose some friends in this new path as well. It's totally okay to grieve those friendships. Remember that when you let go of people, places and things, you are actually making room for new to enter your life.

IT'S OKAY TO MISS ALCOHOL AND NOT WANT IT BACK IN YOUR LIFE

Here is a real mindblower that will happen to you, if it has not already. You are going to miss alcohol and, simultaneously, not want it back in your life. And that is okay.

I notice this contradiction in my sober life. It happened while participating in AA, and it also happened with my therapist, my friends and even with Matthew. I would share that I missed alcohol and automatically get met with a prevention plan, concern and the question, "When are you going to drink?" Sometimes I wouldn't even get to finish the sentence. And I allowed it.

Never once while explaining my feelings did I ever say I was going to drink. I just said that I missed it. They weren't listening to what I was saying, which I did not like. Clearly, being dismissed and not being heard is a trigger for me. In doing work on myself, like the stuff I am coaching you to do, I found out this was one of my triggers. It goes back to my childhood. I have worked hard in the last ten years to use my voice to say, "Please don't cut me off and let me finish." BOOM MOTHERFUCKERS! Seriously, that takes a lot of work for people who have been conditioned to think it's not about them. (When you get to this point in your road, send me a DM on Instagram, and share your victory with me.)

I understood everyone's concerns, but I believe our loved ones have to leave some room for those letting go of alcohol to express themselves without jumping on their backs with step work, prevention plans and daily phone calls out of concern. This overconcern could even push a person away. Getting sober means working your ass off and showing up every day, and instead of realizing you are a human with feelings, your loved ones may discount all the work you have done to get to this point. A sober person could shutdown out of defeat and drink.

If this happens to you, breathe through it and educate the other person, because in all honesty, they don't know. Share with them that it's part of the process, that it may sound silly to them but you did have a relationship and you are grieving it. Let them know you aren't in any jeopardy of drinking because you have these thoughts, and if it does come to that point, you will reach out for help. The people supporting you don't want you to go back to drinking because they care, and . . . there could be a codependency issue on their end. I wasn't kidding about the layers and layers of sobriety and recovery.

It is part of the human experience to go through the process of grieving the relationship with alcohol and miss what once was. You are not a robot. Feel it and be honest. I GET IT! I lived in this space for a very long time, and it comes up from time to time in different ways still. For example, like wanting to know how Bravo celebrities' alcoholic drinks taste. I was not kidding about my love for that network and the people who make up the Bravo universe. So, I ask my friends who do drink and understand the same love to let me know how it is. That, "Awe, I wish I could try it and be a normal drinker but I can't," feeling lasts for less than a minute. But just because I have this thought does not mean I am going to take alcohol to the face and start pounding Loverboy or Bluestone Manor Bourbon. It is the same when you no longer have a partner or friend in your life . . . of course we all think of them from time to time and wonder how they are doing, but it does not mean you are going to invite them back into your life.

When you start expressing your feelings and thoughts in this process, first add the disclaimer that you are not going to drink. That way, the people who you are expressing concern to do not kneejerk and stop listening so they can insert their fears and send you rehab center information via text. It is a boundary you are setting up front. You still may be met with concern, and that's okay because you are loved.

I know I am going against the grain here in the recovery space by discussing this. No one talks about it. It's like alcohol and the life you once lived should all be forgotten about. I do not feel like that is the productive way to go. Forgetting is pretending that it never happened, and it so did.

If I listened to everything I was told not to do or feel while on my road to sobriety, I would still be sitting in my house with anxiety. I didn't get sober just to continue to act like I was in my drinking days but without the alcohol. This is not to say I did not listen to people—because I did!— but I also had to figure out what was best for me and my path. So, yes, I went back to bartending the second year of my sobriety. I was told not to do it because it would lead me back to drinking. Yes, I got plenty of lip about a recovering alcoholic bartending. I saw everyone's point. But their fears then instilled that same fear into me. I was nervous AF that first shift . . . borderline terrified. When I got my groove back during those hours of working, holding alcohol didn't make me want it at all. I was fine. I was empowered and felt so much better doing that one shift than working at my current job in the medical field at a pain clinic. I eventually left the medical field because bartending led me to creating and pursuing my passion in building Sober Vibes. If I had listened to people back then, I would not be here today writing this book. I bartended from year two of my sobriety to the last week of my thirties. I spent eight years sober, pouring drinks, slinging cheeseburgers, growing a business and continuing to show people that just because you're sober doesn't mean you're dead. It's amazing what happens when you continue to trust yourself and not the opinions of others.

COACH TIP

In the moments of living in a space of missing alcohol and not wanting it back in your life, always remember how far you have come, the work you have put in and the time you have spent in this healing space. Remember your "why" but also recognize that it's okay to have this thought. This does not mean anything is wrong with you or that you're doing recovery wrong. You may have spent twenty years with alcohol in your life and it became part of your identity. Keep grieving as long as you need to. Let it all sink in. I can't stress enough that it is totally okay to cry, rage-scream in a pillow or not talk to ten people in a day.

HOMEWORK

Write a goodbye letter to alcohol.

Write a goodbye letter to the person you once were in your active relationship with alcohol.

Many years ago, I wrote a goodbye letter to alcohol, and it was healing and something I needed at that time. I hope both these letters help you and you find the powerful healing in this activity. These are your letters, so write whatever is best for you. Do not stress out about it being perfect. This work is another great reminder of why you no longer want alcohol in your life.

HAPPINESS IS WAKING UP WITHOUT A HANGOVER.

SOCIALIZING WITHOUT ALCOHOL

For so many who start their sober journey, socializing and friendships are their top concerns.

How do we socialize and continue to have friends without alcohol? This chapter is dedicated to this topic. Honestly, it's one of my favorite subjects to teach and talk about, because it is possible. I am living proof of it, and I have used all the methods and tools I am about to share here.

People hold themselves back from quitting drinking because they fear that their social life will be over after they quit. I was one of those and I have heard from so many who feel the same way.

Staying true to the vibe of this book, I am going to shoot you straight for a minute. Yes, you can still have a social life living alcohol-free, but it will look and feel different. Will you still be sitting in a bar 'til two o'clock in the morning or sitting around a campfire 'til midnight with the neighbors who are on planet Pluto while you sit there stone-cold sober? No. Some of these activities will not align with the person you are now. The energy shifts because you have shifted.

When I say, "planet Pluto," I am referring to the fact that when people get intoxicated, they often repeat themselves, slur, become a different version of themselves, are uncontrollable, talk about shit that does not make sense and lose the natural vibration of themselves. You especially won't want to be around drunk people if their drinking triggers you, particularly if you have a family member or loved one who has an issue with alcohol. That one hits differently.

Is it okay to be around people who drink? Yes, of course, as long it doesn't trigger you. One of my besties who barely drinks had a few beers at a Rod Stewart concert and lost her mind when he sang "Maggie May." I got a kick out of her that evening. (By the way, Rod the Bod puts on a great show, and I was surprised by that man's moves.)

You also may be thinking, "But Courtney, didn't you bartend?" Sure did, but when I went back I did it with boundaries, like working a majority of my shifts during the day. Plus, here is the kicker: It is not my place to judge anyone who drinks. Just because a person drinks, I do not assume they have a problem, and as stated before, other people can drink but I cannot. My brain is different.

So how do you do it? Keep reading and you will find out all my secrets.

TAKE A THIRTY-DAY SOCIALIZING BREAK

Say what!? Yes, if you have not taken a little break from the social scene, I want you to think about doing it. If during those first thirty to sixty days you have done this, then perfection. If you have not, please take it into consideration. As you have read, I totally took a break from socializing those first few months. I had to sit still since a lot of my drinking was done out of the house. I had to detach from the social scene, my friends and family for a bit. It was not isolating; I want to make that clear in case you were wondering. It was really me taking a step back, which I believe we all need when it comes to quitting drinking alcohol and going through the first ninety days.

I had a friend say to me when I told her I quit drinking, "Is that why you haven't wanted to do anything and hang out with me?" Yes, absolutely it was. I needed to just focus on me and get through the hard parts without the influence of others. I was extremely wrapped up with my friends and the scene for a very long time. It was time to just focus on what was best for me and that was not to be around it.

Maybe this rings true to you. So if you have passed the thirty-to-sixty day mark and have yet to take a break from the social scene and feel like you need to, do it. It serves as a reset and a detox. Taking this break now will only help you in the future with long-term sobriety.

Think of sobriety as a muscle. You have to do some things you don't want to do daily to achieve and sustain the muscle. This is how sobriety is. You must work on it daily.

Why take a break? Two reasons.

One, I want you not to be tempted and get some sober time under your belt. So many rush to hang with friends and go out and continue to keep doing the same things they were doing in their drinking days. What happens is, they end up relapsing, they say fuck it and they cave because they are not ready. Many use the escape of the social scene to keep them "busy" so they will not have to sit still and deal with themselves. Sitting still means they have to deal with thoughts and feelings. It's okay if you are one of those. Quite frankly, it's common for so many but it doesn't have to continue to be a part of your story.

Two, I want you to be able to sit still with yourself! Sure do.

You honestly may have been conditioned this way since you were a child. Always having to be doing something. Maybe your parents could not sit still and thought having you in twenty-five activities was doing the right thing.

Everyone's nervous system needs a break, and especially during this period, your nervous system will need one sooner or later.

COACH TIP

Do not be afraid to say NO. No is a complete sentence and a boundary. If you have friends who are not taking NO for an answer when they ask you to hang out, keep sticking to it. I know not everyone wants to share right off the riff that they quit drinking, and I respect it, so here are a few different ways to respond to people who ask you to hang out during this time:

- Thank you for the invite, but unfortunately I am going to have to pass tonight.
- Thank you for the invite, but I am staying in for the next thirty days doing a little detox.
- Thank you for the invite, but I am doing a spend-no-money month challenge.
- Thank you for the invite, but I recently quit drinking, and I need to take some time for myself right now. I'm sure you have questions, as I just laid that one on you, and in time, I will share more.

I really like the last one as it is honest, but I understand not everyone is there. The more honest you are, the freer of a person you become in your sober life.

SIXTY-MINUTE RULE

You are ready to paint the town pink; you have sat still for some time now getting through the last few months and are ready to put on your cha-cha pumps and put yourself back into the scene—whatever that scene may be to you. It may be work events, going to dinner with friends, going to a baseball game, going to a birthday party or hanging with the moms and dads after the kids' travel soccer game.

You get the idea.

But before this event happens, your mind starts going down the rabbit hole. The anxiety starts to kick in and the assumptions of how the night will go just start coming at you. The anxiety of people asking you what you want to drink and catching on that you're only drinking a soda pop makes you sweat under your armpits. If this starts happening, take some deep breaths. Breathe in for four breaths and out for four breaths, and repeat this five times. Say this mantra to yourself after you're done with your breathing exercise: "I'm exactly where I need to be right now." It really helps. Remind yourself that you aren't there yet, and you have no clue how the night will go because you have not done this yet in your new sober skin. Also, you know you will be okay because you have this secret weapon in your back pocket.

The secret weapon is what I call the Sixty-Minute Rule.

Before explaining what the SMR is, let me share with you what happened when I started to reintroduce myself back into the scene during my first year of sobriety.

I remember when I said yes to going out to happy hour with coworkers. Yes, happy hour is very much influenced by drinking, but you can also eat and socialize for a bit. So, I finally said yes because I was feeling confident I'd be able to participate. I went, I had a great time, ate some wings, slammed a few Cokes and then totally outstayed my comfort zone. Because I felt like I needed to stay until the end. No one said I had to of course, it was just the pressure and unrealistic expectations I put on myself.

I stayed while my coworkers started to reach that point of being on planet Pluto. I shit you not, a jumbo fishbowl-like drink was ordered with about ten straws in it. They passed it around the table, and guess where it landed? Right in front of me. Then my boss loudly said, "NOOOOO, she can't have that!" Of course, all eyes were on me with the jumbo cocktail in front of me with straws pointed in the direction of my mouth. I picked up the ridiculous drink and passed it to the person to the right of me and said it's okay. I continued to sit there in discomfort, and the anxiety rose and rose. I felt like I wanted to burst into tears. I sat in that feeling for at least an hour, not wanting to make anyone uncomfortable or be the "dramatic, sensitive sober person." I stayed even though I wanted to crawl out of my skin because I was a people pleaser. It was always about them and not me.

I left as soon as someone said they had to go. I got into my car and burst into tears and cried all the way home for a solid twenty minutes. What is fucked up here is that I did this again a month later. That time there was no fishbowl drink incident. But I just stayed past my comfort zone. I would soon learn that it did not matter if I was with friends, family or coworkers—I needed to start respecting my boundaries. My physical and emotional comfort in social situations became a priority for me. This is when I created the Sixty-Minute Rule. It has helped me not go into complete fight-or-flight mode when leaving social gatherings or bawl my eyes out on the way home.

The Sixty-Minute Rule is when you give yourself sixty minutes at a social gathering.

Why sixty? Because it's enough time to show up, be present and leave before you start pushing your threshold. It is plenty of time to socialize before people start orbiting Pluto.

It is plenty of time to put yourself out there, mingle and enjoy it, and then leave feeling good about yourself. You actually aren't bawling on your way home thinking you are the problem.

It is also a good amount of time to help you not think it's rude to leave an event. If you have ever thought leaving early is rude, trust me this thought is common. You might see signs of people pleasing in yourself. Totally something to work on down the road.

You also do not have to say goodbye to everyone at the social event. Seriously, learn from my experience on this one. When I first started dating my husband, we would go to family events, and when it was time to go, the man would say goodbye to his parents and dip out. I would always say, "Matthew, you have to say goodbye to everyone." He of course would then explain that it was too much as he came from an extremely large family and he was not saying goodbye to forty people. I started to see the man's point as I would say goodbye to everyone. He was right. It would take at least another thirty to forty-five minutes to get out the door. I took a page out of my husband's book and applied this to the Sixty-Minute Rule. I said goodbye to the people I needed to at events and dipped the fuck out.

Why is this so important to do in an environment where people are drinking? Because people who have been drinking want you to stay. From their perspective and state of mind, it is the best goddamn event they have attended! And of course, they are going to ask you to stay about two to three more times before you have to respond sternly, and then it gets awkward. When this happens, guess who starts feeling bad and feeling like they are not being respected? YOU . . . not them.

Think about how many times you probably did this to someone who had to leave an event while you had a couple of cocktails in you. I bet you pressured them to stay, disrespected their boundaries and told them they will be missing out if they left. You want to know who the queen of this was? Me! I did this multiple times. When you are under the influence of alcohol, everything goes out the window. There are no rules for an uncontrollable substance.

What if you are having a good time and want to stay past the sixty-minute mark? Then please stay and enjoy yourself. Push your next time marker thirty minutes up. Feeling good and wanting to stay longer? Keep moving the time up until you're ready to leave.

The rule can apply to parties, dinners, receptions, events, concerts, family holidays, really anything. With this rule you are continuing to engage in life and putting yourself out there in a way that feels best for you.

Being a sober bartender for many years, I have great perspective on this as someone who was once a drinker and now isn't. And as the drinking increases through the night, I know that nothing good will come from it. It was the same song and dance at every event. People getting loud, people close-talking, people smelling of sweat and booze . . . and it always ended with at least one or two extremely intoxicated people needing help to the car or finding shoes, purse or their partners. Seriously, it always looked the same! Sharing this with you is me telling you that you are not missing out on anything. I understand that FOMO comes into play, but really, what are you missing out on besides a hangover and the continued shame of what your drinking did to you? You win every time you pick another day sober.

COACH TIP

When you are ready to leave and people ask why, tell them whatever you want. Sometimes little white lies are needed, and that is okay. You do not have to sit there and tell people it's because you are feeling triggered and about to have an anxiety attack. You will be met with a person who has zero boundaries and does not get it at all. Explaining to people who are currently drinking never wins. I have an early morning, I have a headache, I have to go pick up my kid, I have other plans after this . . . all are wonderful excuses.

HOW TO SOCIALIZE WITH FRIENDS

Hanging out with friends once you quit drinking is still going to happen. It just might not look the same as it did when you were in your active state with alcohol. You can still hang out with friends once you get sober.

You can start by creating something new within your friend circle that they might appreciate more than you know. Once you start opening up to friends about your relationship with alcohol and how you are on this sober journey, you will start hearing, "I have questioned my relationship with alcohol." SERIOUSLY. You may even have friends down the road come ask you for help and ask how you got sober. So very, very common.

I have had numerous friends in the last ten years quit drinking and ask me how I did it. It is crazy but also a sign of the times. People do not want to keep numbing themselves and not living up to their best selves. I also believe there is a shift with parenting, and more and more parents want to be fully present with their kids. An awakening has been happening the last few years when it comes to living more mindfully, intentionally and healthily while breaking generational patterns.

When you have someone reach out to you about getting sober, shoot me a message on Instagram and share with me. I am going to say "I told you so" in the best possible way! Your story will help someone else.

But going back to socializing with your pals: How else can you hang with them when you don't want to do the same things you used to do together? You suggest something different. That is right, friend, you continue to be the change. You suggest breakfast. You suggest a movie. You suggest a hike. You suggest a pottery class. You suggest an exercise class followed by grabbing a smoothie after. People who drink after working out are missing the point, and I used to be one of them, sure was. I would smoke cigs and get drinks after working out with my trainer . . . hello, defeating the purpose of optimal health and feeling our best. I would also show up hungover.

You will face some friends who will suggest continuing to do the same thing that you have always done or who won't do these new things with you and that's okay. Their loss not yours. You have other people in your life who will grab a coffee instead of a cocktail. The power is within you to create how you want to show up during this time and still continue to do some living in this process.

COACH TIP

Stop giving your energy to people in your circle, whether they are friends or family, who don't care. If they are the ones who don't invite you to things anymore when you quit drinking or don't ever try to do something with you that doesn't involve a happy hour, fuck them. I'm sure this coach tip is a little jarring, but it's true. If they are acting this way now, are they really a friend? By not giving them your energy anymore, you are protecting yourself from further disappointment down the road. Continue to protect your energy from people who continue to show you who they are.

N/A BEVERAGES

One of the many benefits of getting sober right now is the amount of goodness that is the N/A beverage space. "N/A" is nonalcoholic. There is now a slew of mocktails, N/A beers (not just O'Doul's!), N/A wines, N/A spirits and unlimited flavored sparkling waters, pops and coffee drinks.

N/A beverages are a hot topic, especially in the recovery world. And I hope one day this space will support and recognize that what matters is staying sober each day, and that how you got there is your business. Some will tell you that drinking an N/A beverage will lead you down a road of relapse. Some will say it is fine and N/As really helped them quit drinking. Two opposite ends of the spectrum. I will always support what makes you happy.

N/As are extremely useful for people on the sober path, especially when it comes to socializing. These options can help you feel comfortable and included when out and about. I will also add that water, soda pop and coffee provide the same comfort as well. The only people who will call you out for what you are drinking are most likely people with their own drinking issues. Again, my friend, I have observed a lot over the years and I was one of those. Insert winking emoji.

During my bartending days, I had many people come to the bar and ask me to pour their N/A beer in a glass, ask me to make a drink that looked like a cocktail or even ask me to put a piece of fruit on the side of the glass of their Diet Coke. I will tell you that no one noticed that these were not alcohol. The boom of N/A beverages is needed, and I am excited for you and the community about all the choices people have now.

You know how cool it is to go into restaurants and see a mocktail menu or different N/A beers? Inclusion for all is awesome; give me a little shoulder shake.

When I quit drinking, there were just a few N/A beers on the market, and I would drink them if we were out. Matthew would always say to me, "Do you think you should drink those; I heard it could lead to relapse." At the time, Matthew was seeing a therapist who brought this up to him. I stuck by what made me feel good and the fact I enjoyed one or two when we were out (if the establishment had them of course). I would have some and he would not.

Fun fact, my husband now LOVES all the N/A beer options.

The thing is, it was no one's business to tell me what I should or shouldn't do. I had to continue to fail forward in my path. I had to figure out what was best for me as I figured life out being alcohol free.

COACH TIP

My disclaimer for this topic is always: If the N/A world of beers, mocktails, wines and spirits triggers you, do not drink them. Do not feel like they are a necessity. Here is a little secret: I cannot do the N/A wines. They are a little too close for comfort for me. So, I don't drink them. Simple. If I can find one that does not hit close to home, then I'm sure I would enjoy it, but for now, I stay away.

During the holidays, I have a fun little tradition where I drink some cranberry/Sprite or ginger ale in a wine glass. It's festive and there is nothing wrong about drinking from a pretty glass.

Also, get comfortable with iced tea, soda pop, water and coffee. Not all places have the N/A options yet. Drinking hot water with lemon is perfectly acceptable and comfortable in public places.

LISTEN TO YOUR MIND, BODY AND SOUL

One of the most important tips I am going to share with you is in this section when it comes to navigating how to socialize alcohol free.

Yes, after reading this chapter, you will have the tools you need to socialize alcohol free. However, if you ignore that gut feeling you get that's saying you've reached your threshold and have socialized enough . . . you feel tired or even like you want to crawl out of your skin . . . it could trigger relapse.

Ignoring these signs in your body is only going to lead to disaster. These signs can show up a few different ways. Anxiety, an uneasy feeling or even your body entering fight-or-flight mode.

Hear me out. You wake up on a Saturday morning feeling great, but as the day goes on, you experience some anxiety or fear. You may not even know exactly what you are experiencing, but you know that you are beginning to dread even the thought of going out. You may even feel triggered to drink. The idea of drinking sounds delicious and becomes more and more overwhelming. Something inside you tells you that staying home would be better, but you don't want to cancel on friends because you want to show the world, I'M SOBER AND I CAN DO THIS, and you just bought the best pair of pumps. (They were a nice gift to yourself after being ninety days sober. And you should celebrate these milestones with something fancy, whatever fancy is to you!)

Is it totally normal that this will happen to you? One thousand percent. It's so common. You might just wake up feeling like this. If your body is speaking to you, it's okay to take a knee.

There is no shame here. None. It also doesn't mean you're weak. You are healing, and it's so important to keep protecting your energy and self in sobriety. Pushing past these feelings and ignoring them could end in relapse for you. Pay attention to the feelings and do not ignore them. It is up to you to decide what you can and cannot handle.

HOWEVER—there is a however in this situation—I know this may sound conflicting, but I still want you to try to work through these feelings. Are you psyching yourself out or really feeling uneasy and having this reaction? Have you gone out once this week already and maybe two events in one week are too much for you? Have you gotten plenty of sleep? Are you about to start your cycle? Or are you just feeling very triggered today? Because I want you to thrive and be able to participate, and 85 percent of the time you will. These cues from your body are signs that more self-care and self-love are needed. Listen to them.

In my years of sobriety, I have sat out on many events. I used to be very hard on myself about it because I felt like I needed to perform and please others. I felt like I was disappointing people if I didn't show. In time, I grew and learned to understand how I operate as a human and when I need more self-care. I understood that I was an empath, extrovert/introvert (yes you can be both), enneagram number three . . . and here is a big one for women: I understood that I experienced the highest levels of anxiety around my cycle.

Since I worked with the public for so long, I knew when it was time to decompress from the world. With clarity in sobriety, I understood how I moved and have accepted this is part of who I am. I understood as time went on not to double-book my social calendar every day. I understood that if I worked five days in a row, I would not be participating with humans on my first day off. I understood that I needed to protect my energy. I understood that if I needed to cancel plans the day of, that was okay as well. Because the people who I canceled on were ride-or-dies and did not make me feel guilty.

This past year, I was invited to a surprise birthday party. I was jazzed for it all week. The day of, I woke up on my menses, anxiety was induced and I started dreading the event that was at 7:30 p.m. Around noon, I was ignoring the signs and continued to push through. I was also six months postpartum and still sleep-deprived. But goddamn was I going to make this party. I left my house, got in my car, started driving and was halfway there when the anxiety kicked in full force. I had to pull over and try to breathe through the anxiety attack and the racing thoughts of how I was wearing a grandma sweater and how the girls I was going to see that night were going to be dressed to the nines, and look, here comes postpartum-sweaty-grandma-sweater-wearing-feeling-Shrek-like Courtney.

I caught my breath, called my husband and said, " I am picking up a pizza and coming home." He was very supportive and said, "You tried." I said, "You're goddamn right I tried." And I felt instantly better because I was going home. At thirty-nine and a few months shy of being ten years sober, I had that feeling. Yes, I could have trucked through, but when you are in that heightened state and comparing yourself to Shrek, how enjoyable will the experience be, anyway?

I wish I had these tools during the first ninety days so I could have transitioned so much smoother with the understanding that I had options, especially the option of not being so hard on myself during this process. I want that for you. Use these tools; they help. You cannot avoid your life and events you are committed to. I understand that. Some people have work commitments, and I get that happy hours are necessary for careers. Or that you must attend kids' parties with parents who are all about the mommy and daddy drinking culture. Or that you and your friends have a standing Saturday social hang. I get it all. You now have tools to tweak these events, to accommodate them around who you are today without alcohol.

You can listen to the Sober Vibes podcast; I share a lot of episodes about socializing alcohol free, and I even did an episode in season three about my experience of ignoring myself that night in my grandma sweater.

It's also totally okay to say no to things when you get invited to places.

COACH TIP

Stop fighting who you are. Yes, stop the mindfuck. You are made up of so many wonderful qualities. Let them shine. You operate how you do because, layer by layer, this is how you were built. In the last few years, I got into the enneagram personality test. This really helped me understand myself so much better than any other personality test out there. It's spot-on and wicked accurate. You can even see how you vibe with different personalities. I suggest taking the test. Just Google it and a test will come up.

Also, learning whether you are an introvert or extrovert is a huge nugget of knowledge that can help you understand what you need as a human. Once you know, you can also plan according to your response to others and filling your tank.

HOMEWORK

List three times you held yourself back from quitting drinking because you feared losing your social life and friends. Describe the moment and the feelings that went along with it.

When will a thirty-day socializing detox happen? Pick a date and record it here. Then, come back to this and write out what happened. How was the thirty-day socializing detox challenging? What did you learn and how did it help you? Anything you noticed that you didn't notice before? Write it and reflect.

Practice responding to a person who asks you to hang out. Write out the conversation here.

Practice responding to a person when they ask if you want a drink. Write out the conversation here.

What events, gatherings or family parties will you use the sixty-minute rule for? List five that this rule will help with.

N/A beverages . . . will you try them or are they off limits for you? Write why either way.

Have you ignored feelings of anxiety that come up when you feel like you to need to be at all the social events when you didn't even want to go at all? Write about a time and describe the physical and emotional feelings that arose.

Moving forward, how will you schedule your week when it comes to social events? Is there way to cut back or add to it? How are you going to balance right now so you are not pushed over the edge?

SOBRIETY IS A JOURNEY, NOT A DESTINATION.

LIVING A
SOBER LIFESTYLE

Courtney, I made it to the last chapter, now what?

You continue to keep on truckin' day in day out, not drinking alcohol.

I have found many people who enter this lifestyle find that they think sobriety is a place. That they get past the first sixty or ninety days and think that they have arrived and it's all good. They think they are, or at least should be, cured. Once again, I will be the fun police and let you know this isn't the case. There is no arrival to sobriety; it is a continuous journey. I have used a lot of these words in this book: journey, process, healing, recovery and path. And that's because these are what you will be experiencing for the rest of your days in sober life.

How have I made it through ten-plus years of sobriety? I never stopped respecting it and searching for long-term serenity. The one time I stopped respecting sobriety was when my son was born, and I was completely thrown out of the routine I created in my sobriety. Something I respected and understood. I started getting wonky. The thoughts of alcohol were at the forefront. What did I do to turn it around? I got back into my groove and started respecting the process again. I jumped back into my daily gratitude, personal development and meditation. I relearned life and how to do it with a child. I sought help in the avenues of my life that I desperately needed help with, like hiring a sleep coach for my son. I let go of ego and realized I needed help. I eventually even joined an expert food coach's membership to help me relearn about nutrition for myself. I had to get back to things that made me feel good. Because during those first five months with my son, drinking started to sound good again.

None of us have this completely figured out, but what we do have figured out is what works best for us to not drink each day. Yes, in time you will not think about drinking at all, and then something happens and your world is completely turned upside down. A baby, a divorce, a death, a job loss, a pandemic . . . anything that can just totally rock you. That sleep deprivation was insanity for me. Looking back at it all seems like a dream, but even in the fog of it, I had to dig deep and remember WHY I gave up drinking in the first place, and now I had the baby I dreamed of for years. Was I going to let this moment take me down or was I going to rise? I chose to rise.

RELAPSE

What happens if you relapse? I recently read *Anti-Time Management* by Richie Norton and in it, he says, "Every sunset is an opportunity to reset. Every sunrise begins with new eyes." If you do relapse (because realistically, people who enter sobriety and recovery have a very high chance of relapsing that first year), remember it took me four years to get to the point of being good and tired. Talk to anyone on this path and the majority of them will tell you the same thing. You might even hear someone say, "Yeah, I was sober for five, ten, twelve years and went out."

If you relapse, I want you to reset at sunset.

Learn from the bump in your journey. What did it show you? Where did it take you? Where do you want to go from here? The power is always within you and in how you look at the opportunity. Will you rise above and move forward? Or will you need to learn a few more times that alcohol no longer fits into your life?

- Learn from it, forgive yourself and move forward.
- Learn from it, forgive yourself and move forward.
- Learn from it, forgive yourself and move forward.

A lot of people have asked me whether they should start their number over once they relapse and are back to day one. My answer is, "Do what works for you." Some people don't count their days, some do. Some will tell you that you must start back at day one if you relapsed. I tell you to never forget the time you had before the relapse. You were doing and living the sober life. None of that time gets swept under the rug and forgotten because you could not handle the pain of miscarrying a child at five months or your mother dying unexpectedly or discovering your partner has a second family in Nebraska.

You just do not know what life will throw your way, and everyone handles emotional trauma differently. When the world shut down in 2020, we had some of the highest rates of alcohol use, overdoses and deaths due to drugs and alcohol of all time. It's no surprise, as so many of us were stripped of our routines, structures and jobs, while also dealing with racial injustice and an aggressive amount of stress all over the world. So yes, escaping reality was set high.

It's important after coming out of a relapse to look at different ways of finding support and help. Maybe you got sober and did it on your own. Now is the time to look back and reflect and start trying something a little differently this time. Like seeing a therapist, trying meetings, hiring a coach, being more open to others about your sobriety, finding a hobby and/or starting meditation.

You have to keep chipping away until you find the package that works for you. It is like building safety nets around you to help prevent a fall. Find your safety nets.

COACH TIP

If you relapse, it is important to remember your new "why" of not drinking. Oh, yes! Get to thinking. Your "why" from six months to five years ago is going to be different than today's. You change, life changes and it is a whole new situation. Dig deep and connect to your new "why." Also, make a new sober plan going forward. Maybe you have not tried meetings before, and it's time to see if that avenue helps. Or maybe a therapist can finally start helping you work through past trauma.

SHAME

I have not really gone into detail about shame, but I have mentioned it in this book. Shame will keep you sick. Shame will keep you stuck. Shame will eat you alive. At some point in your sobriety and the healing process you embark on, you must start letting go and forgiving. Changed action is an apology to yourself. If you are living in your sober life, why keep holding on so tightly to actions you once did years ago? You don't need to keep beating yourself up for behaviors you're not living in anymore. Now, if you keep repeating the same behaviors, then yes, nothing has changed, but I know it has for you.

COACH TIP

A wonderful way to start letting go of shame is through journaling. Releasing the shame onto the page means you are no longer carrying it. You probably have an event that happened during your drinking days that maybe only one person knows about. Or you drove drunk with the kids once. Or you cheated on your spouse. Or you just have shame because you never thought you would be like your alcoholic father. Whatever shame you carry, it's time to release it. Journal it, write it out and then burn those pages.

You may even take it a step further, and as I recommended, if you have an apology to make towards a person or an amend, then start now. Do not do them all at once. Give yourself time to process in-between. That in-between is going to help you recognize that you closed that chapter with the person you wronged during your active relationship with alcohol. With the apology comes another release. The release of some stale-ass shame that's been carried around for years; it's a beautiful thing.

Seriously, this works. As I did my amends, it was an instant twenty-five pounds off my chest. I have also journaled and burned the pages around things in my drinking days that I have never admitted to anyone before. I have forgiven, released and moved on.

Stop with the narrative that you are this terrible person. The more you can practice grace and forgiveness with yourself, the more you can then practice it on people you need to forgive. Once you start, the shame dwindles.

I have stated that, to this day, the thing I regret most that always makes my eye twitch are the times I drove drunk. Lately, I have been really trying to work on this because, clearly, I have attached shame to it. Here I am ten years later, and I still haven't forgiven myself for this. Well, the time has come, and I'm no longer going to live with this feeling and attachment because it doesn't serve me anymore.

We have all heard of families of crime victims who forgive the person who killed their daughter or son. How they say holding on to that hate no longer serves them and how letting go of hatred sets them free because that hate only hurts them more.

The same goes for you in this process. I know you have done some very fucked-up things, but you aren't doing those things anymore. Forgive and let go of the shame . . . a little each day.

HOW TO KEEP CONNECTED TO NOT DRINKING

On my ten-year sober birthday, I shared this on social media:

> TEN mother fucking years sober!
>
> I have been looking forward to this birthday because ten years is the amount of time I spent in my active addiction to alcohol, and now it's been ten years in my Sobriety. I like the balance. It is the Libra in me. Because I've spent ten years in Sobriety doesn't mean 'I'm safe' and allow my ego to take over and stop respecting my Sobriety. I plant myself even firmer in my program and continue life, one day at a time.
>
> I woke up humbled this morning. I allowed myself to play a tape in my head like a rewind. If I continued to drink alcohol, where would I be? I saw no child, no husband, no cat, no self-love, no inner peace, no sober vibes, no friends/family . . . the list goes on. I saw continued chaos, loneliness, despair, depression, hangovers and

ultimately what would have led me to an early death. That is the power of what ONE choice in your life will make. I am a statistic, and it's around 30-ish percent of people who enter Sobriety/Recovery will stay sober the rest of their lives . . . that's insane. That number tells me we have got to do better in helping people with long-term recovery. I promise to continue to help in that fight. I remember one of my first meetings, and a man said he had been sober for ten years, and I thought to myself, goddamn, how will I ever make it as I was on day five . . . It will be harder before it gets easier, but Sobriety is the greatest gift you can give yourself.

The most important message I want you to take from this is this tool I used: I allowed myself all these years to keep connected with my practice on Sundays to reflect on how it was when I drank. I did not forget. I allowed myself, with love, to peek in a dark window of my past with sober eyes of what life was like.

Allow this. Do not forget. Use it for fuel . . . of where you never want to be again.

I do believe with all my heart and soul that doing this practice allowed me to keep moving forward living an alcohol-free life.

COACH TIP

Pick a day each week to do this practice. Reflect in a meditative state, journal or look back at pictures of yourself while you were in your active drinking days. Pick a day-after scenario where you had a terrible fallout after a night of drinking. Feel it. Allow it. Breathe it in for a few minutes. After you are done with this practice, say to yourself, "I forgive myself."

By doing this, you will also be doing a mental rehearsal for where you never want to live again. It is a real two-for-one practice that only takes a few minutes once a week.

LIVING IN ALIGNMENT

There will come a point when you get to the ninety-plus day mark and start to feel the living-in-alignment perspective. Alignment can be defined as arrangement in a straight line. This is going to be you in sober life. You are going to want to live in alignment with your soul and what you need. The alignment you live will not match the alignment you were once in. Shit changes, mainly you.

What you once loved doing in an alcohol-induced state no longer serves you in this clear-headed road you are on. You will feel this as time passes and certain situations get brought up. That is why it is okay to let go of old friends, places and old limiting beliefs that no longer serve you. We were not put on planet Earth to not evolve.

Keep aligned with what makes you feel good in this new path. Do the things that help you daily. Do things that bring you joy. Ditch the assholes. Love the real ones. Celebrate your victories. Give yourself grace. Practice gratitude. Allow rest. Allow adventure. Allow abundance. Keep LIVIN' in your sober alignment.

COACH TIP

Of course, your road in sobriety will never be straight; it will be filled with ups and downs. It's important during these ups and downs to stay in alignment, which really means staying true to yourself. Remember to keep moving forward no matter the setback.

Just because I'm wrapping up this book doesn't mean your sobriety is over. Let us do a quick recap of all you've learned.

- **Section One:** Quitting drinking. Remember to talk with a doctor before you quit drinking. Ask for help and find support that vibes with you. You are not alone. Help and support are all around.
- **Section Two:** Little by little, it all adds up. Stop the overwhelm. Stop the mindfuck. How much fun were you really having during your active cycle with alcohol? It is crucial to build a new, healthy routine. Find things to do that make you feel good.
- **Section Three:** Let it out! Grieve alcohol and who you once were. It's okay to cry when needed. Keep remembering your "why." The Sixty-Minute Rule is going to be your new best friend. Never forget where alcohol always led you. Keep choosing the sober life one day at a time.

Thank you for allowing me to be part of your story and allowing me to coach you through your first ninety days of sobriety.

For the days you do not believe in you, remember that I do. I am so proud of you for making it this far. You deserve everything and more. You are worth the fight in the days you feel like you have got nothing left.

Please, when life gets hard for you (because it is an ebb and flow), always rise up.

Choose you, choose the alcohol-free life. It is a road that is not easy but one that is worth it every step of the way.

XOXO,

Courtney

HOMEWORK

Write it out one more time: Why are you choosing not to drink anymore?

_____

_____

_____

_____

_____

_____

_____

_____

_____

_____

_____

_____

_____

_____

_____

_____

_____

_____

_____

_____

_____

_____

_____

_____

What is your relapse prevention plan?

What shame are you continuing to carry around with you?

How can you start forgiving yourself?

Describe an event from your drinking days that you reflect on in a positive way as you continue to move forward.

How will you stay in alignment going forward in your sober journey?

Now that you made it ninety days sober, how are you feeling?

Reflect on and share what you have learned these last ninety days.

RESOURCES

SOBER VIBES FREE RESOURCES

www.courtneyrecovered.com

Under Resources section:

- Sober Vibes Morning and Night Routine Workbook
- Feeling Fit and Fun in Sobriety Workshop Series
- What's the #1 Threat to Your Sobriety Quiz
- Sober Vibes, women-only Facebook group
- Sober Vibes Mocktail Guide
- Sober Vibes Sober Not Boring Calendar
- Sober Vibes Meetings—The Fix

WORK WITH ME

www.courtneyrecovered.com

Under Work with Me section:

- 30-Day Coaching Program, BREAKTHROUGH
- Next Level Sober Support, 8-Week Coaching Program
- 1:1 Mentorship for 3 to 12 Months

Speaking and Consulting Inquiries: sobervibes@gmail.com

Sober Vibes Podcast: iTunes, Spotify or your favorite podcast app
Website: www.courtneyrecovered.com
Instagram: @sober.vibes
Facebook: @sobervibes
TikTok: @sobervibesofficial
Pinterest: @sobervibes
LinkedIn: @sobervibes

LET'S CONNECT

If you enjoyed this book, please share with me on Instagram! I would love to chat with you about it, and see how this book impacted you.

RECOMMENDED BOOKS

Personal development has helped me in so many ways on this road. Here are my recommendations to help you along your road of life:

Set Boundaries, Find Peace: A Guide to Reclaiming Yourself by Nedra Glover Tawwab

Codependent No More: How to Stop Controlling Others and Start Caring for Yourself by Melody Beattie

Drinking: A Love Story by Caroline Knapp

You Are a Badass: How to Stop Doubting Your Greatness and Start Living an Awesome Life by Jen Sincero

The Four Agreements: A Practical Guide to Personal Freedom by Don Miguel Ruiz

You Can Heal Your Life by Louise Hay

It Didn't Start with You: How Inherited Family Trauma Shapes Who We Are and How to End the Cycle by Mark Wolynn

The Road Back to You: An Enneagram Journey to Self-Discovery by Ian Morgan Cron and Suzanne Stabile

The Universe Has Your Back: Transform Fear to Faith by Gabrielle Bernstein

The 5AM Club: Own Your Morning, Elevate Your Life by Robin Sharma

Atomic Habits: An Easy & Proven Way to Build Good Habits & Break Bad Ones by James Clear

The 5 Second Rule: Transform Your Life, Work, and Confidence with Everyday Courage by Mel Robbins

I Thought It Was Just Me (but it isn't): Making the Journey from "What Will People Think?" to "I Am Enough" by Brené Brown, Ph.D., L.M.S.W.

ACKNOWLEDGMENTS

I must first start off by saying I am so grateful each and every day to be sober. For what was a scary, unknown journey became the most beautiful surprise of my life. Without my sobriety none of what I have now (especially this book) would be possible. The many gifts of sobriety always deliver.

Thank you to the universe for continuing to lead the way.

To my husband, there are no words to express my gratitude for you. You have supported and believed in me when no one else did. You have always wanted the best for me even when I did not see it or think I deserved it. Thank you for your continued pep talks, even if they had to do with Henry Ford and how many cars he had to make before making the Model T. I picked up what you were laying down in the times I needed it the most. Thank you for navigating the first year-plus of parenthood with me as I wrote this book. Thank you for being you. I love you, Matthew.

To my Fiona, your little soul was brought into my life for a reason. You were rescued from the streets, and the universe placed you in our home. I did not know that an eight-pound, four-legged friend would be the bridge to my sobriety journey. You continued to show me what unconditional love and forgiveness was over the last ten plus years. You have been by my side through the good, the bad and the ugly. You even cuddled up with me as I wrote this book. Never far away, you are and will always be the promise I made that day.

To my son, the day I had you, I changed instantly. You have given me the love I never knew was possible. You have made my heart grow infinitely. You make me fearless. You have made me see that limiting beliefs are nonsense. You are my game changer. Thank you for showing me what really is important in life and to always believe in miracles, because you are mine.

To my Sissy, what a ride. I love you, UJ June with all my heart and soul. Thank goodness I have you in this thing called life. It would be such a bore otherwise. I am happy we do not get hammered anymore, fistfight and catch cases. Sorry about that one, Kimmie.

To Mom, Dad and B., thank you for supporting me in my sobriety. I know I caused some sleepless nights, and now as a parent I can empathize with how that would be. Sorry for those nights and I love you.

To the rest of my family, thank you for the continued years of support.

To my friends, I love you all so very much. I cannot express how much it has meant to me that you have supported me. You never gave up even if you had to protect yourselves and place boundaries in my drinking years. I appreciate the last ten-plus years of meeting me where I was in this journey of healing and recovery. You guys are the real ones.

To my Grandma Pullen and Grandma Shirley, thank you for showing me what strong-ass women were made of. Thank you for guiding me and always being around me.

To my editor, Franny, and the team at Page Street Publishing Company, thank you so much for taking a chance on me and fulfilling a lifelong dream of mine.

To my therapists, coaches, mentors, favorite bands, movies, shows, authors, Stevie Nicks and Oprah: you all have helped me in times of need, THANK YOU.

To the Sober Vibes community, thank you for allowing me to help you along your journey of sobriety and recovery. You have tuned-in and listened to the podcast, followed the Sober Vibes social media pages and have even trusted me to coach you along your alcohol-free journey. I love you; you have given me a voice in ways I didn't know was needed and continued to give me opportunities to help you. Forever grateful.

No one does this road alone; support comes from many and the people who have impacted and imprinted your life along the way. My hope for this book is that it impacts and helps you in your life. You can always call me a friend.

MONDAYS ARE A LOT MORE PLEASANT WHEN YOU DON'T BINGE DRINK THE ENTIRE WEEKEND.

ABOUT THE AUTHOR

Courtney Andersen is a podcast host, author and sober life coach who has helped countless people quit drinking and thrive in sobriety. Courtney is the founder of National Sober Day (9/14) and founder of the online community Sober Vibes.

Courtney is a wife, mother, lover of coffee, believer in Karma, a personal development junkie, a Disney adult, someone who thrives from funny people and is straight addicted to the Bravo Network.

30 DAYS OF SOBER ACTIVITIES

1	2	3
CLEAN YOUR HOME	GO FOR A WALK	GO TO A MOVIE
7	**8**	**9**
GO TO BREAKFAST	GO TO A MEETING	TAKE A BUBBLE BATH
13	**14**	**15**
ORGANIZE A ROOM	BINGE WATCH A NEW SERIES	GO FOR A HIKE
19	**20**	**21**
SLEEP AND REST ALL DAY	HOST A SOBER DINNER PARTY	DE-CLUTTER YOUR HOME
25	**25**	**27**
GO TO THE ZOO	VOLUNTEER TO BABYSIT FAMILY OR FRIEND'S KIDS	GO FOR A COUNTRY DRIVE AND CRANK THOSE TUNES

4 GET A MESSAGE	**5** READ A BOOK	**6** DIY CRAFTING
10 START A MEDITATION PRACTICE	**11** CALL A FAMILY/FRIEND TO CATCH UP	**12** SIGN UP FOR A YOGA CLASS
16 LEARN HOW TO PAINT	**17** TRY BAKING COOKIES FROM SCRATCH	**18** GO SHOPPING FOR A DAY
22 SIGN UP FOR A GYM MEMBERSHIP	**23** GRAB COFFEE WITH A FRIEND	**24** VOLUNTEER YOUR TIME
28 GO TO A CONCERT	**29** GO TO A PLAY/MUSICAL	**30** CLEAN THE FRIDGE